CUT, PASTE, CREATE

1,000 Images to Cut Out & Collage

Flanzella

ilex

Biodiversity Heritage Library: 35, 39, 45; iStock: 3DSculptor 97, Alberto Gagliardi 87, Alberto Masnovo 79, 97, Aleksandr Kharitonov 93, Alhontess 77, Andrea_Hill 105, Andrei Apoev 73, Anton Vierietin 53, 53, Arkady Margolin 45, ArtBalitskiy 53, 71, 71, 91, 93, 97, Arthit_Longwilai 81, atlantic-kid 43, barsrsind 73, bauhaus1000 27, 31, bembodesign 81, ben phillips 79, Bhupi 61, Bkamprath 119, Boris_Zec 123, carol_woodcock 79, Chorna Olena 139, clu 41, 59, 85, 89, CSA-Archive 105, CSA Images 9, 133 31, 39, 41, 43, 49, 51, 53, 59, 61, 63, 65, 67, 77, 83, 85, 87, 91, 93, 97, 99, 105, 125, CSA-Printstock 31, 43, 53, 55, 57, 59, 61, 63, 67, 77, 79, 87, 89, 93, 97 image 10, 97, 101, 105, 141, dageldog 39, Deagreez 65, Delmaine Donson 59, Diamond Dogs 57, dima_zel 97, dubassy 55, duncan1890 35, 37, 41, 51, 55, 63, 69, 75, 99, 101, 103, 105, Ekaterina Balashova 73, Elena Kanakhina 45, fairywong 109, firina 23, 25, 113, Galina Sviryiaeva 67, George Marks 49, 51, 65, Grafissimo 43, 101, Gwengoat 111, Gyro 77, hadynyah 63, Hanna Udod 43, Hein Nouwens 27, ikryannikovgmailcom 69, ilbusca 37, 85, 89, IMOGI 81, ivan-96 27, 31, izusek 57, jacobeukman 121, janniwet 83, jeffwqc 49, JohnnyChing 97, JohnnyGreig 59, johnwoodcock 27, Kangah 51, KaterinaKr 67, kathykonkle 43, KrivoTIFF 87, Krzysztof12 79, ksmitho808 105 la_balaur 67, lenta 143, leonid li 93, LiiaLonnArt 87, Man_Half-tube 99, Margarita Balashova 135, Margarita Kharkova 67, Maria Sonia Salvador Verdugo 81, master1305 129, MattGrove91, Max5799 43, Mayur Kakade 61, mehmettorlak 45, mihtiander 133, mmello 27, Moonstone Images 105, mubai 69, 71, 71, Muhammad Afaq 85, mychadre77 45, Nastasic 89, Nerthuz 97, NSA Digital Archive 23, 25, 27, 31, 51, 55, 57, 61, 71, 79, 87, 95, oersin 45 , OLGA MELNIKOVA 45, Olga_Korneeva 23, 25, paseven 105, PeopleImages 57, PepeLaguarda 51, Petchjira 11, 79, Pituk Loonhong 83, PoppyPixels 133, ReinStudio 55, RetroAtelier 63, RG-vc 81, RogerBradley 117, Sabrina Bracher 63, Slavica 81, spb2015 67, Srdjan Stefanovic 79, Stefan_Alfonso 77, 89, Sviatlana Barchan 67, TamakiKou 107, Tamiris6 33, Tatyana Goncharuk 89, Tempura 55, The Naturalist 23, The Nature Notes 31, 39, THEPALMER 31, thomas-bethge 101, TinaFields 115, Tom Kelley Archive 13r, 49, 51, 53, 55, 57, 59, 61, 63, 65, 83, 87, 89, 93, 127, Tuba Acik 85, Vac1 45, vatrushka67 69, vector_ann67, vectorartnow 73, Victoria_Novak 43, Viktoriia Raznatovska 67, Whiteway 79, wyoosumran 5, yarn 85, Yayasya 27, Yuliia Kostenko 89; Leah Flanagan: 14a, 14b, 15a, 15b, 16a, 16b, 17, 18, 19a, 19b; Library of Congress Prints and Photographs Division Washington, D.C.: 91, 93, 95, 99, 101, Carol M. Highsmith's America 91; NASA: JSC 97; Pexels: Alexazabache 91, Anete Lusina 83, Cottonbro 63, Josh Hild 91, koolshooters 35, Matthiaszomer 91, Padrinan 89, Pixabay 89, 91, 93, Quintingellar 91, Reneterp 83, Shukran 91; Rawpixel: 23, 25, 17, 29, 35, 37, 39, 41, 47, 49, 51, 65, 77, 89, 101, 103, 137; Rijksmuseum Amsterdam: Purchased with the support of the F.G. Waller-Fonds 55; Shutterstock: AKaiser 99, Alexander_P 99, Antti Heikkinen 111, Bamidor 89, EliaLady 45, himmahdesigns 91, Hseena 89, Ines Behrens-Kunkel 45, Julio Jodan 91, ledokolua 93, PitukTV 83, Rawpixel.com 61, 63, 77, 91, 95, 103, 105, Sanit Fuangnakhon 45, Thitisan 95; Smithsonian American Art Museum: Gift of Chicago Society of Etchers 27, Transfer from the National Museum of American History, Division of Graphic Arts, Smithsonian Institution 99; Wellcome Collection: 23, 25, 27, 29, 31, 37, 41, 45, 47, 55, 57, 63, 65, 95.

First published in Great Britain in 2026 by Ilex,
an imprint of
Octopus Publishing Group Ltd
Carmelite House
50 Victoria Embankment
London EC4Y 0DZ
www.octopusbooks.co.uk

An Hachette UK Company
www.hachette.co.uk

The authorized representative in the EEA is Hachette Ireland, 8 Castlecourt Centre, Dublin 15, D15 XTP3, Ireland (email: info@hbgi.ie)

Distributed in the US by Hachette Book Group, 1290 Avenue of the Americas, 4th and 5th Floors, New York, NY 10104

Distributed in Canada by Canadian Manda Group, 664 Annette St., Toronto, Ontario, Canada M6S 2C8

ISBN: 9781846016615

A CIP catalogue record for this book is available from the British Library.

Printed and bound in China.

10 9 8 7 6 5 4 3 2 1

Commissioning Editor: Emma Hanson
Editor: Rosie Hilton
Art Director: Ben Gardiner
Designer: Isobel Platt
Production Manager: Caroline Alberti

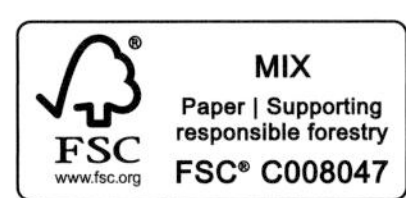

Contents

Introduction 4

Tools & Materials 7
How to Use This Book 8
Quick Technical Tips 10
Quick Spiritual Tips 11
Collage Exercises 12
Gallery of Inspiration 14
1,000 Images to Cut Out & Collage 20

Introduction

Collage is all about communication. It tells a story and it's our job to figure out what that story is. Collage can often spark something within us that we didn't even know was there, connecting our subconscious mind to our conscious one. And I believe that's why it has been life-changing for me.

Fun and reflection are also part of collaging. We may get lost in the process. In fact, many of my students say it's one of the easiest mediums to achieve a flow state in. They'll attempt collage for the first time and a few hours later they find they've created artworks that make them laugh or realize something about themselves.

I am able to make sense of the world around me through collage. For me, it began as a mental playground to escape to, and later became a puzzle that helped me understand the complex world around me. It taught me to seek out beauty in a pile of 'garbage' as I looked for my next image. As you start to collage, you'll begin to see the value in old books, receipts, tickets... anything paper related!

Developing my collage art style has been endlessly interesting. It has helped me learn more about myself than anything else I've ever done. My work is humorous, analogue, talkative and vintage-obsessed – these traits have always been within me, but I had never before had the right medium to express them.

Collage has taught me patience as I have searched to find the right pile of images to transform into a work of art. It has taught me that art is not just about the final piece; it's also about the conversations it might spark and how the viewer interprets it.

My first few high-school yearbooks say I wanted to be a dog walker, perhaps an early sign that I didn't know that 'artist' was an occupation. I wanted to study visual arts at university but was discouraged, so I chose multimedia and communications instead. Throughout the programme and after graduating, well into my career as a graphic designer, I retreated to paper collage as an escape from the digital world and from the stresses of everyday life. For me, collage is a safe space to imagine the unimaginable and to dream. I hope you find it to be a safe space to explore and to take a break from any of your stressors too.

After I'd been doing it for a while, I found that other people were interested in discovering the art of collage, so I started hosting collage clubs. I found comfort and a home in my love of collage art; it stimulated my brain in a way nothing else could, while allowing me to express myself in a new style. After years of quiet pursuit, I registered the name Flanzella, turning my passion into a business in June 2019. I worked every night for years towards this dream until, in 2025, I was able to pursue my art full-time.

Through Flanzella, my goal has always been to inspire people to pursue their art. This book is an extension of that dream: I hope it inspires you on your path to making collages and sharing them with the world. The world needs more collage!

People often question whether or not collage is a form of fine art. I hope that, through increased popularity and awareness, one day it will be recognized as such. Anyone who has tried collage knows there is a true art to it. I hope you discover that in this book, whether you are a seasoned collagist or this is your first collage resource.

Finding images is often one of the longest and most challenging parts of the process. Within the pages of this book you will find an assortment of images – of everything from mushrooms to people to mountains – for you to cut out and use in your collages. I hope this book becomes a staple in your collage practice as it has become in my own. Everyone using this book will have access to the same images to cut out and collage, but how you choose to use them will show just how diverse our imaginations can be.

I'd love to see what you come up with! Tag me on Instagram, @flanzella, or email me at hello@flanzella.com. If you need help with the process of making collage, check out my YouTube channel @Flanzella for tutorials and inspiration.

Good luck, and happy collaging.

Xo,

Leah (Flanzella)

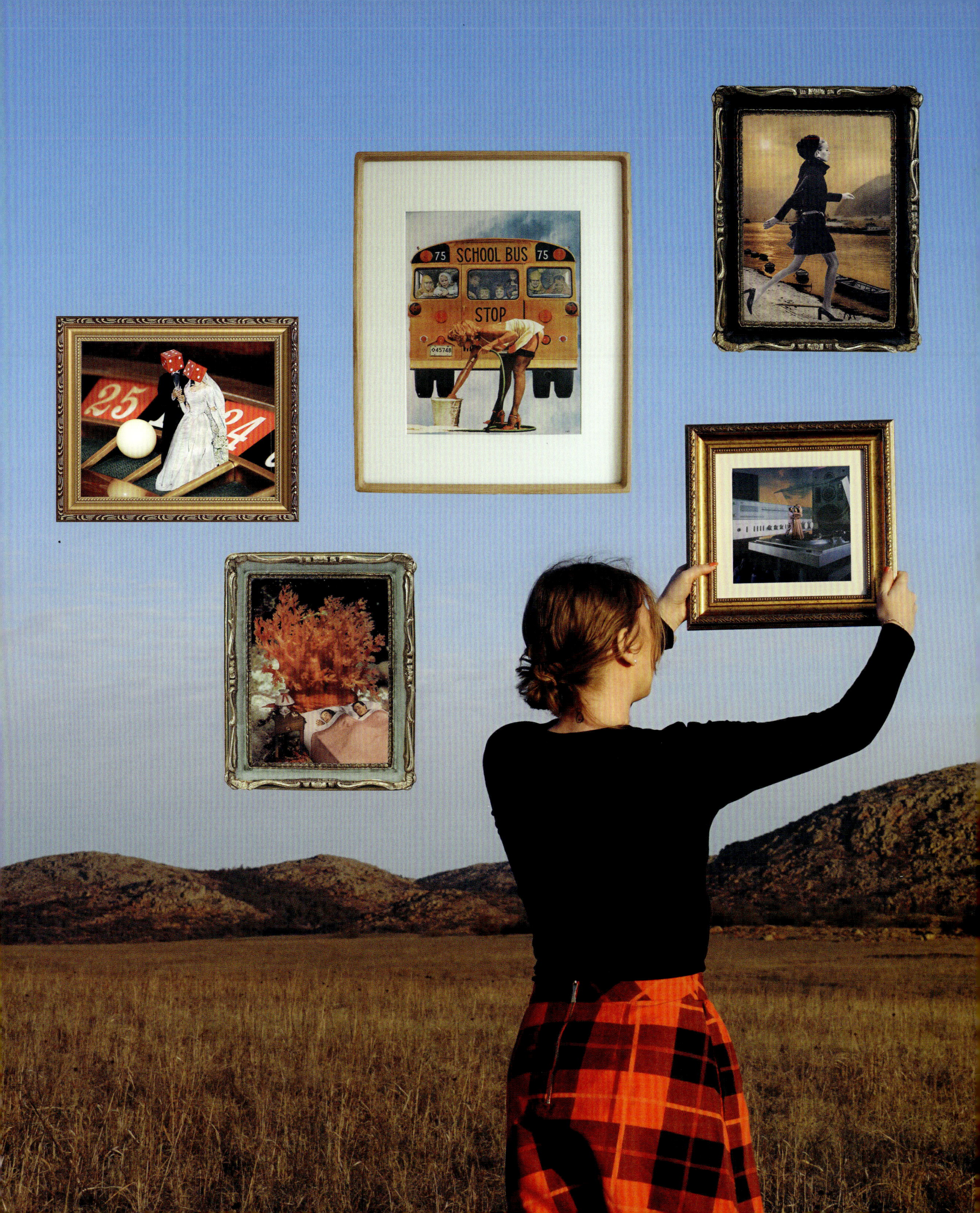

75
SCHOOL BUS
75
STOP
25

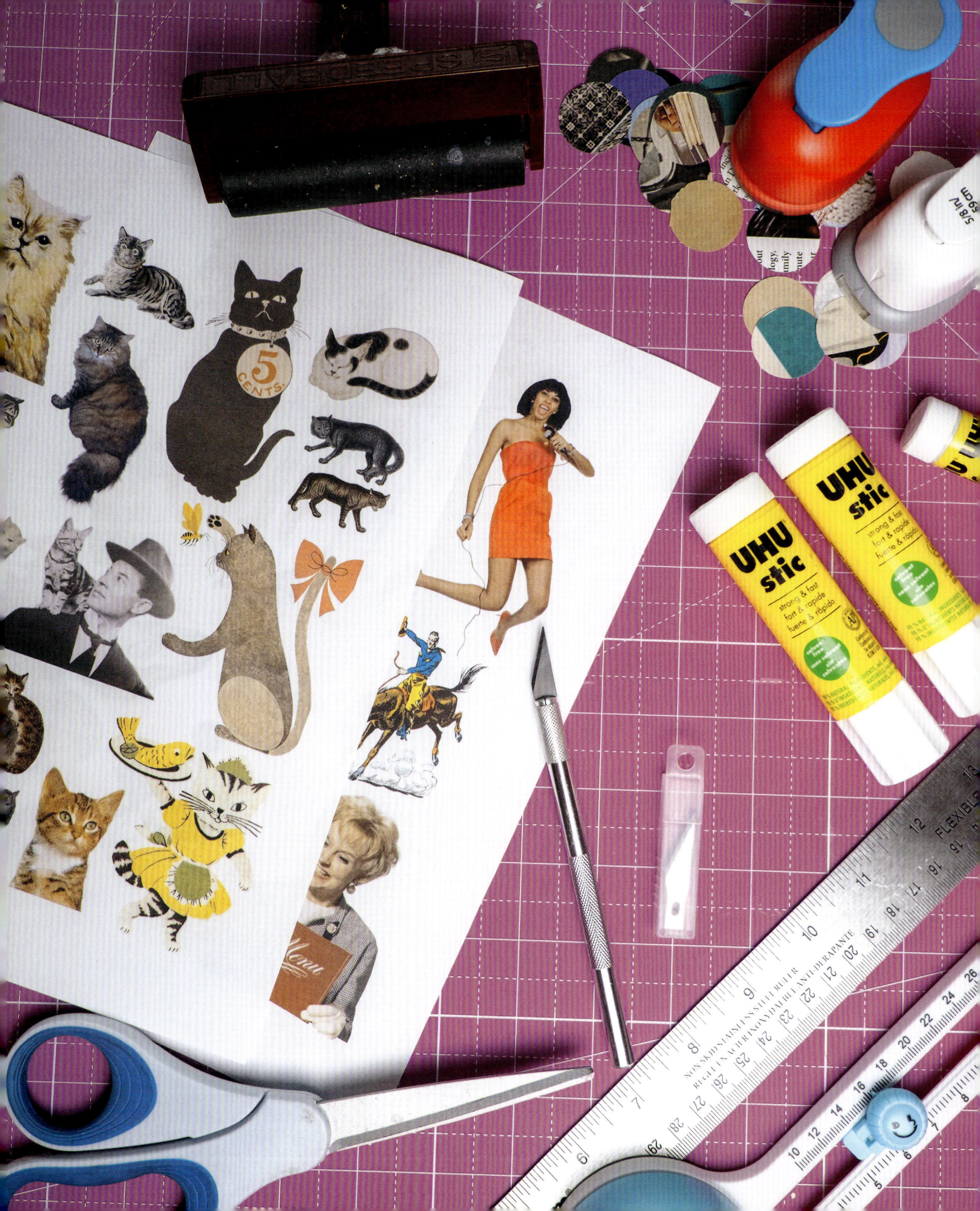
UHU
stic
strong & fast
fort & rapide
fuerte & rápido

Tools & Materials

Craft knife & cutting mat
Don't confuse this with a Stanley® knife or box cutter. A craft knife should be as thin as possible to avoid tearing your paper. Alternatively, for cutting straight lines, use a straight-line cutting tool, which you can get at any craft shop.

For a cutting mat, I recommend something spongy. You can start small but if you choose to do larger works it makes sense to scale up to a larger mat. Always cut on top of your cutting mat so you don't damage other images or your desk.

Craft scissors
I recommend a titanium non-stick blade, which will not get sticky if you get glue on it. Some people like to have multiple sizes of scissors, but I work with just one large pair. I believe the torque of a larger pair of scissors is best for any situation. It does take practice, though. Think of your scissors as your wand: you must learn how to hone their magic over time. I advise practising as much as you can with the same pair, as you will slowly get better at precision. If you find your papers tearing under your scissors, the blade may be too thick or not sharp enough. Try sharpening them or investing in a new pair.

Circle cutters & hole punchers
These are great for making large circles and adding diversity to your shapes. Again, they are available at any good craft shop.

Ruler
I recommend a metal ruler with cork backing: it will prevent slippage and ensure crisp cuts.

Archival-quality glue
In collage, there are many different adhesives to choose from: glue paste, matte medium, glue stick or spray. Personally, I love a glue stick and my favourite is UHU glue, which is readily available at craft and stationery shops.

Archival glue is acid-free, PH-neutral and designed to last a long time without affecting your artwork. If your glue is not archival, over time the pieces will fall off the paper backing or turn yellow from the acid in the glue. Many of my first artworks had this problem. I strongly recommend that you upgrade to archival-quality glue.

Brayer
This is a roller tool that helps to roll the papers onto your substrate without bubbling or crease marks. I recommend a 15cm (6in) one, which can cover more ground than smaller versions. Lightly press the middle of the piece being glued and then use the brayer to flatten one side at a time, working from middle to edge. The key with the brayer (as with many other parts of the collage process) is to move slowly to ensure the paper is stuck down at the right angle, in the right spot.

Archival-quality paper
Although I prefer mixed-media paper to glue my artworks onto, I encourage you to experiment with different paper types. Some artists like texture in their work, others want the flattest paper they can get. Some work on card stock and others on everyday printer paper. I like a medium thickness – I use a 160gsm Canson Multimedia paper, usually 11 x 14in (about 28 x 35.5cm). I find a little grit leads to a stronger adhesion, and excess glue doesn't show up the way it does on flatter paper. The most important aspect of choosing paper, though, is to make sure it is archival quality, meaning it is acid-free. As with non-archival glue (see above), papers containing acid will eventually yellow and affect the colour of your collage.

Some collage artists like to work in a sketchbook to keep their work chronological and tucked away. I recommend this method for beginners, as it's also easier for storage.

Other substrates
Although paper is the most common substrate, you can experiment greatly with other materials. Some of the most popular options are wood, glass, stretched canvas, book covers or cardboard. One of my favourite techniques is to collage onto wood and then seal it with resin. (If you're interested in learning how to do this, there's a tutorial on my YouTube channel, Flanzella.)

Each substrate requires a different technique, so if you are looking to experiment, this could be fun for you!

How to Use This Book: A Step-by-Step Guide to Creating Your Own Collages

There are many ways to collage, but here's what I suggest if you are just starting out.

1. Start by flipping through the pages of this book until you locate a piece you can't take your eyes off.

2. Loosely cut around the image (save cutting out the details for later) and put it right next to the book. Continue to flip to find other images that could go with it. I like to use colour and intuition to navigate this step, but you may prefer to be led by humour, theme or a story you are trying to tell. Refer to the collage exercises on page 12 if you're looking for inspiration for how to get started with selecting images.

3. Once you have a couple of pieces, flip through the backgrounds to see if your collage needs one. Sometimes a plain white background helps the pieces pop more.

4. Now it's time to cut your pieces out in detail. Cut the outside edge with scissors and any 'landlocked' portions with a craft knife on a cutting mat. For small pieces like fingers or plant leaves, I like to skip all the details first time round and then go back to cut them out slowly.

5. Once everything is cut out, it's time to place the pieces where you think is best. Use scale, colour and storytelling to guide you. Ask yourself: what story do I want the viewer to see?

6. Artists often ask themselves, 'When is a piece complete?' It can be a hard question to answer. I like to take away a few pieces and see if what is left still tells the same story. What is needed to say what I want to say? What is not?

7. Once you've decided what can stay and what needs to go, it's time to place and paste. First, and particularly if there are a lot of pieces, take a photo of your composition on your phone so you have a reference point for where everything needs to go. To make pieces look more integrated into the background, use your craft knife and cutting mat to cut slits to nestle the pieces into (as I did in the second collage featured in this book: I cut a line that mimicked waves across the water and then tucked the woman in). Once you've done this, put a piece of scrap paper down so the table doesn't get glue on it, then grab your archival-quality glue and coat the entire back of the first image. Take the gluing process slowly so the papers don't rip, and don't lift the glue stick until you've finished. When starting out, many people glue the papers quickly and in lines away from them. This is a sure recipe for rippage!

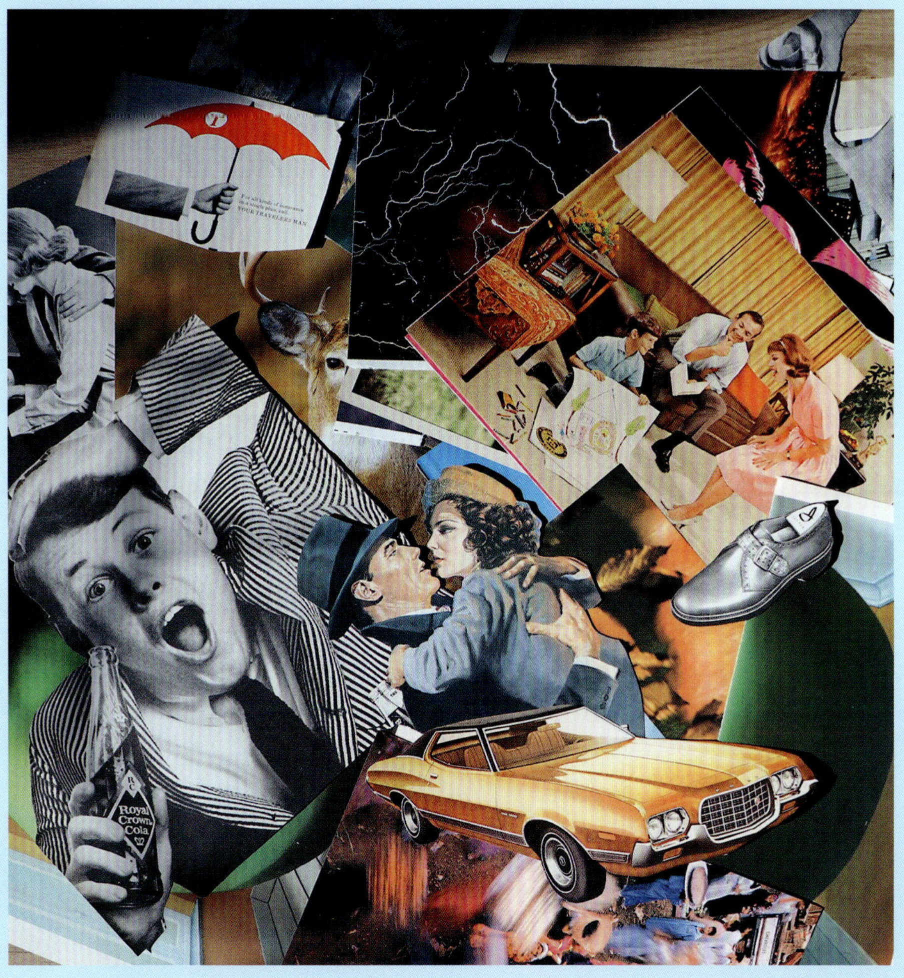

8. Now it's time to place for real. Pick up the piece you just applied glue to and slowly find where it should go on your composition (refer to the photo you took if you need to). Lightly place the piece, holding it at the top and bottom. I like to have only a very small portion at the centre of the image touching the substrate while I ensure it's at the right angle and in the right spot, in case I need to move it over. Once you're happy with the position, grab your brayer and slowly roll outwards from the middle point that is already touching the substrate. Repeat for all the pieces.

Bonus: *If your collage has a lot of pieces, try gluing any overlapping images together before securing them to the background. It's much easier to glue three pieces than it is to glue twenty!*

Congrats! You've made your first collage using this book. You may have pieces left over that you didn't use. I recommend nestling them back in the page you cut them from so that you can find them again later. Some people like to store their papers in a filing cabinet by topic, others use clear bags, some use boxes... This storage part is a whole art of its own and something you will learn over time as you find the best method for you.

Quick Technical Tips for Making Fabulous Collages

1. Use scissors to cut out the perimeter, then use a craft knife for the fine details and trapped space inside the image.

2. Use a craft knife to cut into the background so you can tuck elements in. This will make the piece feel more cohesive.

3. Avoid white edges by cutting on a slight angle. This will ensure the white edge shows on the reverse and not the front.

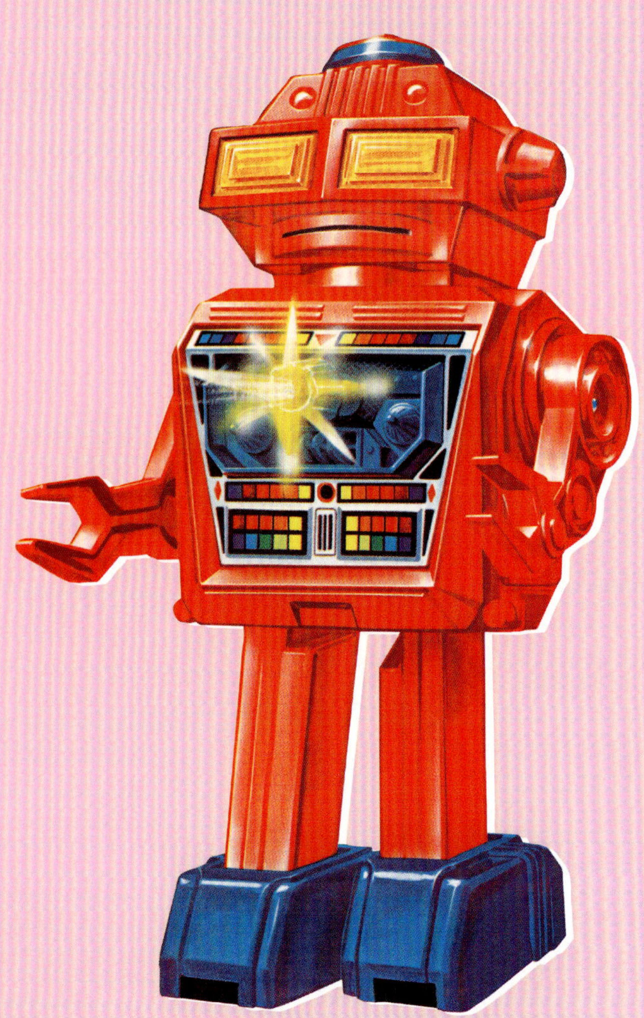

4. Don't push hard with the craft knife. Go over the spot lightly and repeat the same stroke if necessary. Pressing hard can tear the paper.

5. When using a craft knife, it can be easy to run straight over each blade of grass, for example, but those small details are what makes the piece look great. Switch to scissors if they work better for you, or take the time to cut each line.

6. Remember to use a cutting mat under the image you are cutting out so you don't damage your table or the page behind the one you are working on.

7. Move your glue stick slowly when coating your paper in glue, and don't lift it off the paper until you have finished. Pushing down hard and/or lifting the glue stick can lead to the papers ripping. (If the papers still rip when you work gently and slowly, it could be that the glue stick is old or dried up – grab a new one!)

8. Glue your cut-out pieces on some scrap paper so you don't get glue on the table.

9. Use a brayer to minimize bubbles and creases. Move slowly to ensure the paper glues down nice and flat.

Quick Spiritual Tips for Making Fabulous Collages

1. Set the mood to create! Light a candle, put on some music, clear off a nice working area and make sure you have all your tools out before you start. Treat your art time like self-care.

2. Often the images lead you rather than the other way around. With collage, a lot of beginners have an idea in their head and try to reproduce it. This is often very hard to do, since finding the exact image you are looking for can be tricky. Hopefully this book will make it easier for you, but I like to let the images I find guide me instead.

3. Use your intuition to help you create. I often start with colour, finding things that work together tonally, and then work my way into creating a narrative; using pieces with similar undertones can help to make a work look cohesive. Other artists begin with shape, scale or many other things. Over time you will find your own voice. If you need some help with this, try out my collage exercises on page 12.

4. Collage takes patience and imagination. Although a lot of people think of it as a quick art form, it often is not. It can take a long time to find the right pieces, so don't give up!

5. Look for recurring ideas or elements in your work as you continue to create. Often collage can bring out subconscious messages. Remember to take time to look at your artworks and 'read' them. What common themes does your art have?

6. Have fun! Art is not about harsh criticism. The most important part is learning about the art form and about yourself. In a world full of negativity, flood yourself with affirmations and pride while collaging.

7. Lastly, if you have a perfectionist complex, make sure you remind yourself to 'just glue it'! One finished piece is better than a hundred unglued works. Focus on experimentation and play, not on the end results. When I am stuck in this way of thinking, I like to either make the ugliest piece I can, or use my scrap pile to create a collage. Both break me out of this perfectionist loop.

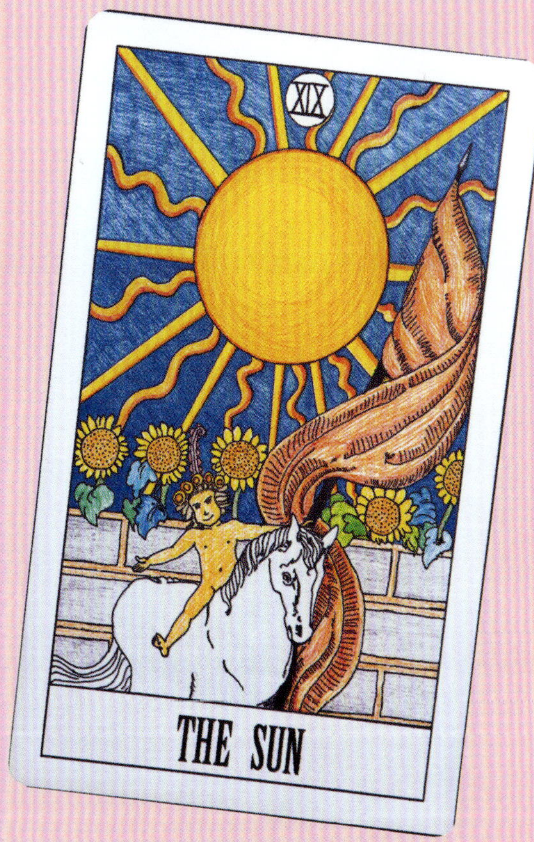

Collage Exercises

Colour exercises

Complementary colours
Pick a colour you like and find a few images in the book with this colour.

Now find its complementary colour on the colour wheel – it will be opposite your first colour. Find a few images with this complementary colour.

Try to make a collage using the pieces you have selected. You will see how the contrast can make an interesting composition and create visual excitement. Refer to the colour wheel if you need help.

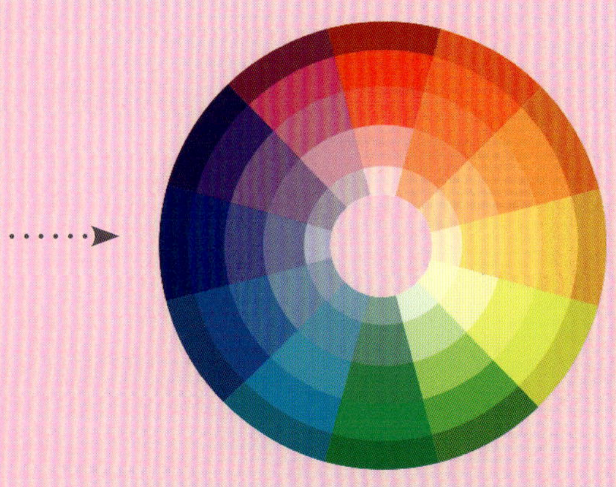

Analogous colours
Pick another colour. Then choose the colour or colours next to it on the colour wheel. These are called 'analogous colours'. See how these images work together in comparison to the complementary-colour exercise, creating a harmonious effect through less contrast.

Scale exercise
Using scale to make a surreal image is a fun technique that collage artists often experiment with.

Start with choosing a background. Now find something to go in the foreground that is way bigger or smaller than it usually is. For example, a giant dog on top of a hill or a woman the same size as a lake.

Prompt-led exercise
Stuck on what to make? Every month I put out a prompt list for my community. A lot of people find it helps to have direction when asked to make something. Here is a list of prompts you can try out:

Spiral	**Singular**	**Movie**
Chair	**Collection**	**Vase**
Hill	**Instrument**	**Envelope**
Electric	**Bag**	**Mattress**
Horse	**Dark pink**	**Bingo**
Slip	**Glow**	**Story book**
Leaves	**Refreshing**	**Lightbulb**
Mythology	**Remix**	**1980s**
Kismet	**Science**	**Denim**
Torn	**Heathen**	**Cowboy**
Indigo	**Sidecar**	**Circus**
Experiment	**Opening**	**Opposites**

The fun part about these prompts is that you can choose one or more and mix them together. Sometimes a prompt can get you started when you're not sure where to begin. That said, sometimes the collage will inspire you to take a new route.

Storytelling exercise
Remember that, as I said earlier, collage is the art form of communication. Your collage should say something. This means picking images that juxtapose one another. Pretend they are having a conversation as you flip through the possibilities.

Ask yourself questions along the way:

- Where is somewhere strange I could put this dinosaur?
- What is this person jumping into?
- Why is the ground lava?
- Who is climbing the mountain?
- How might the story change if you use matching or contrasting furniture?

The possibilities are endless once you start asking yourself questions and letting your imagination run wild. Collage art can be used to tell a story. So, what story are you telling?

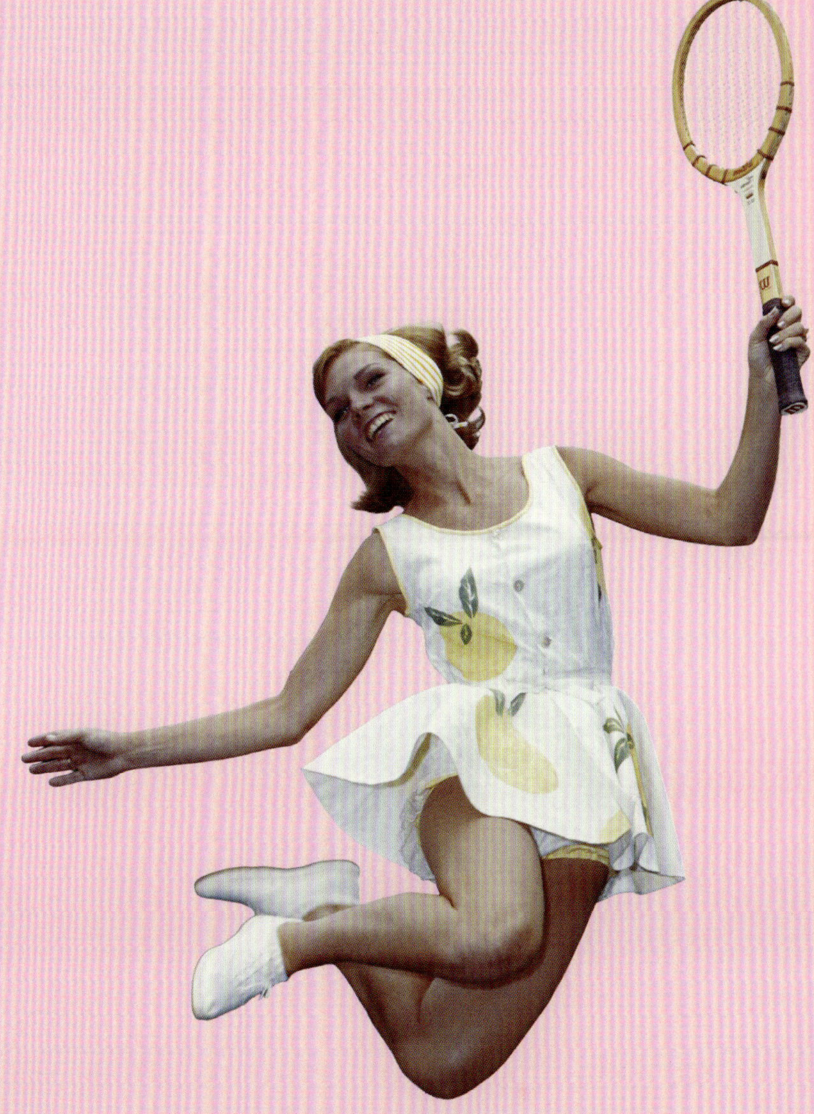

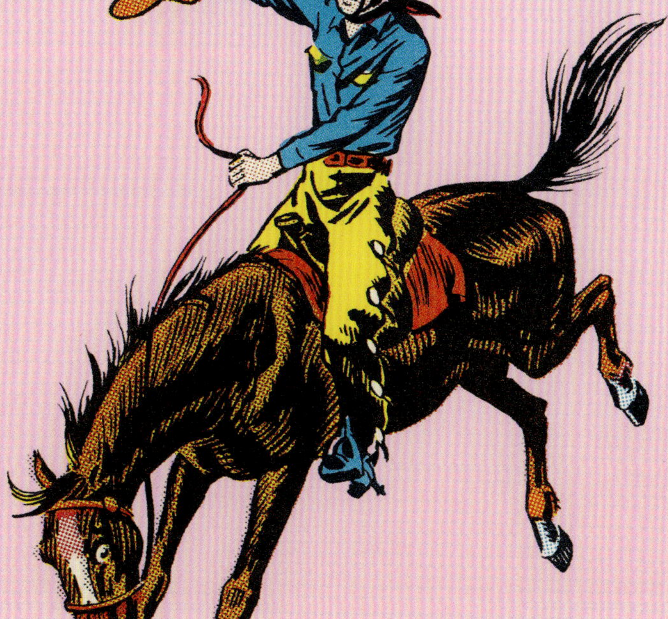

Postcard exercise
Who doesn't love snail mail? I sure do. Imagine getting something in the post that was handmade especially for you!

Cut out a 10 x 15cm (4 x 6in) rectangle in thick paper (I like 300gsm) and use this to collage onto. Then write a letter to a loved one and add their address. Send it to them and wait.

Working at a smaller size can be fun as it's much faster. This approach is also perfect for birthday cards, thank-you cards or just showing someone that you are thinking of them!

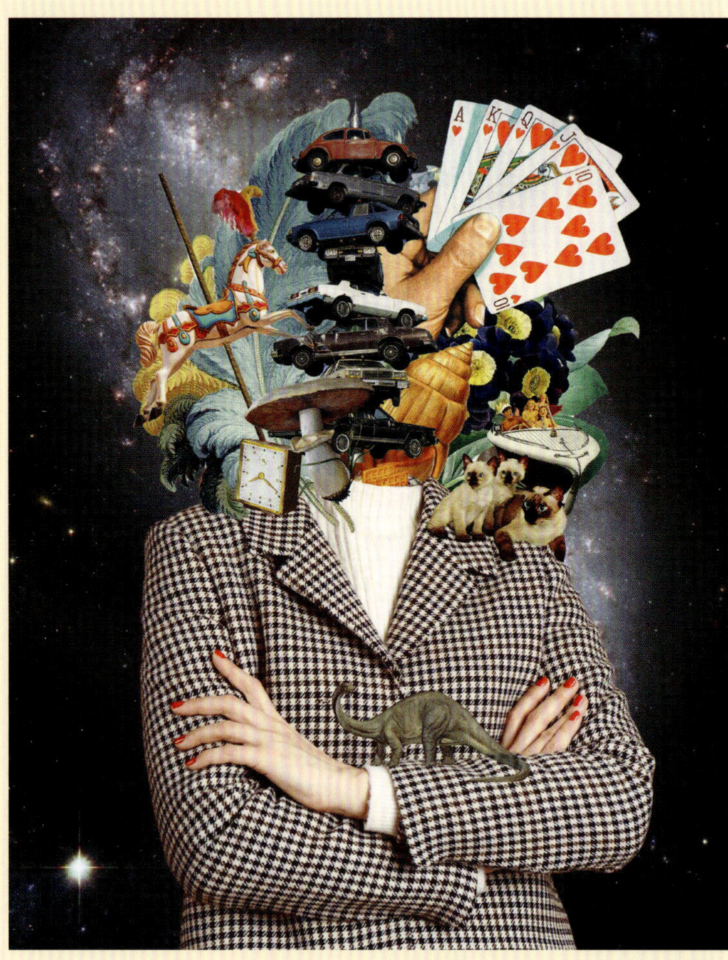

Take a maximalist approach. How many pieces can you fit into a single artwork?

Now try the opposite. How few images can you use to make an artwork?

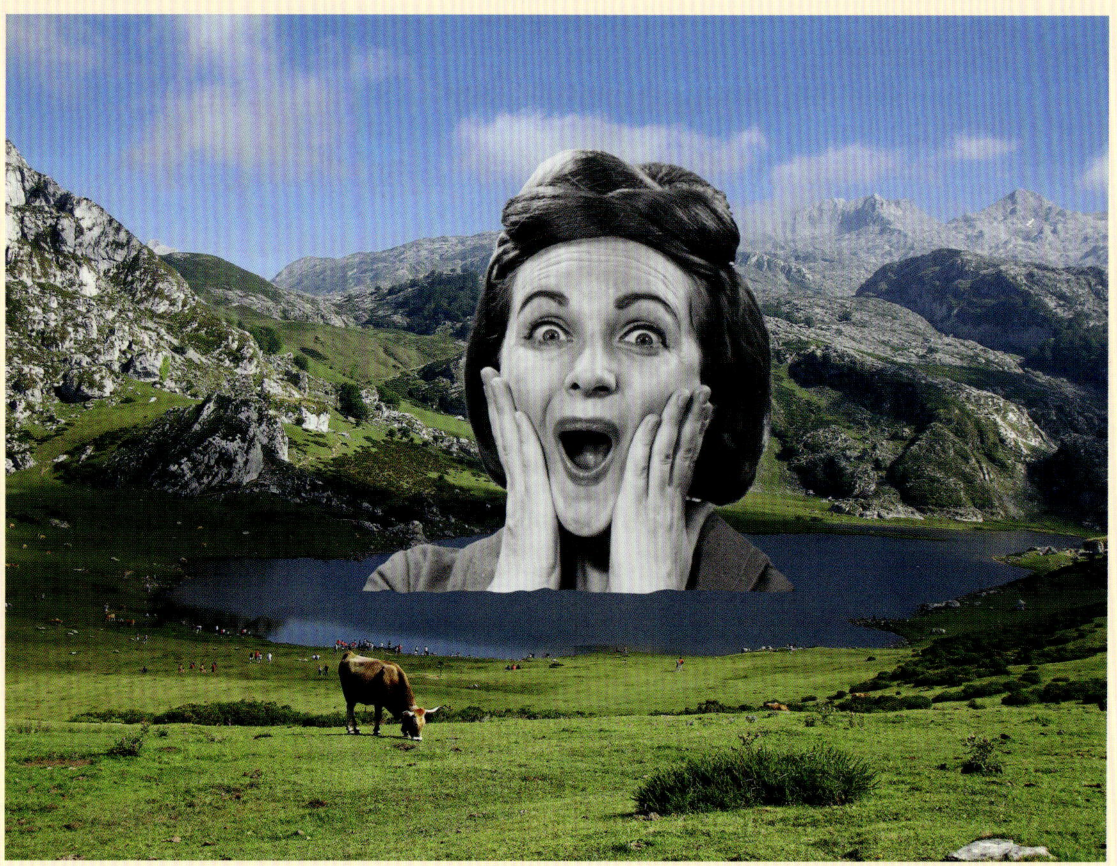

Can you tell a story with just two pieces of paper?

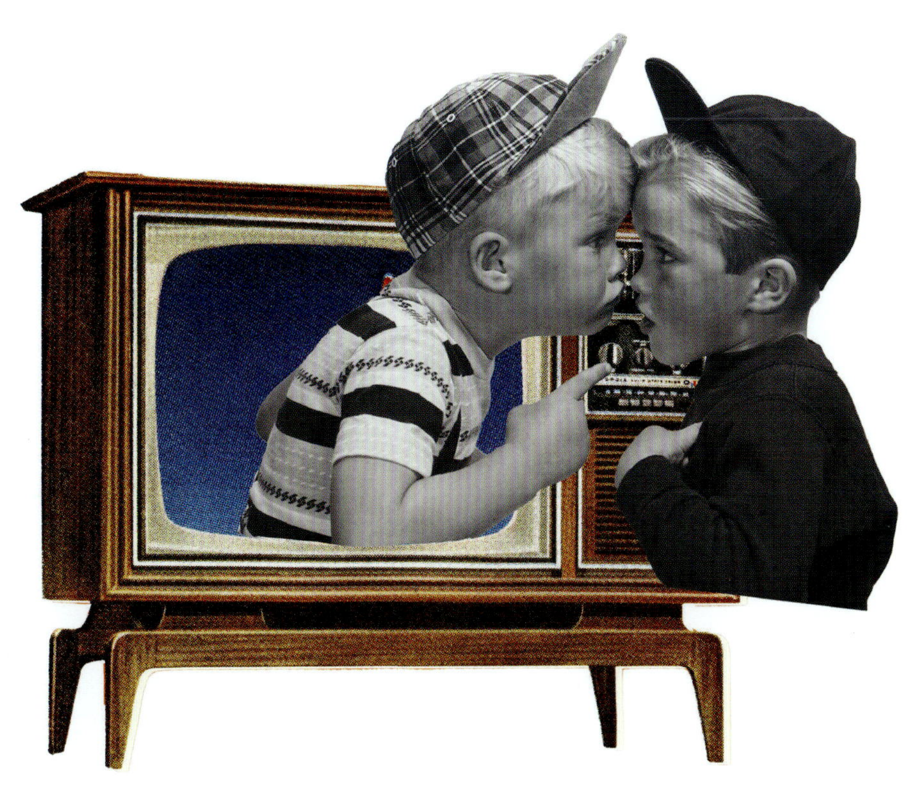

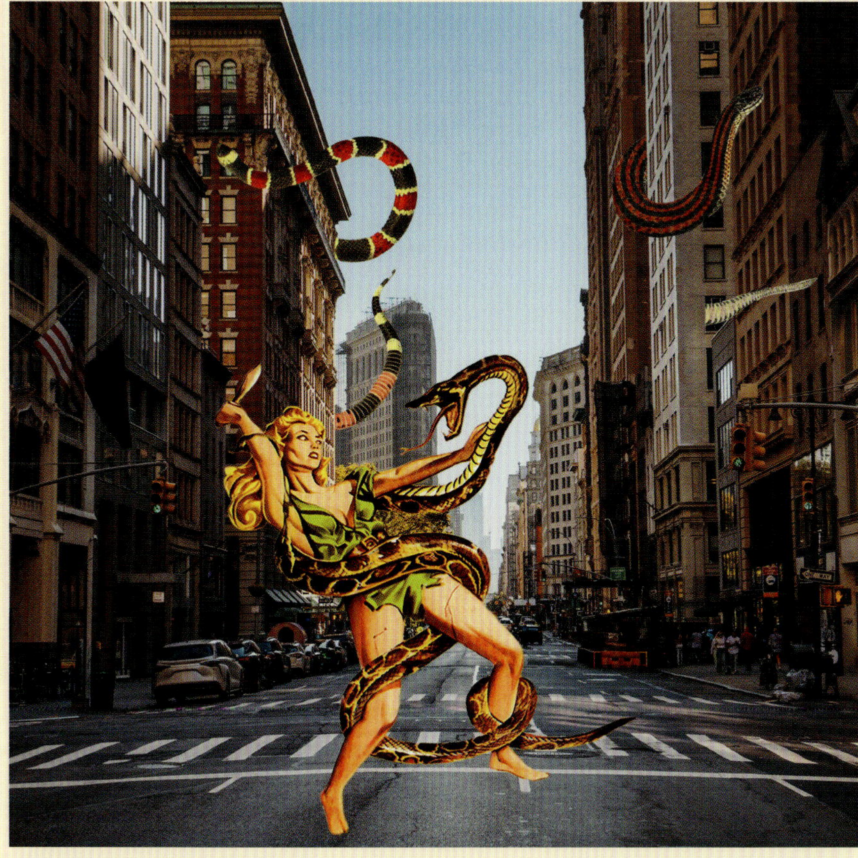

Anything can happen in a collage. What about giant snakes taking over a city?

Contrast is key. Try using a bright background when working with black and white images.

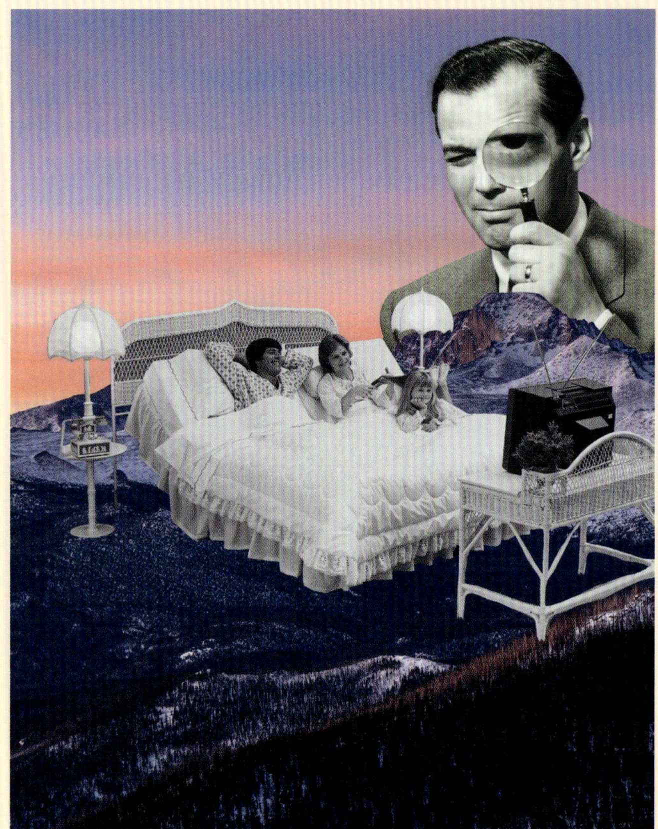

Take your art to a new location. How about under the sea? Up in the stars? In a tree? Collage can take you anywhere your imagination wants to roam.

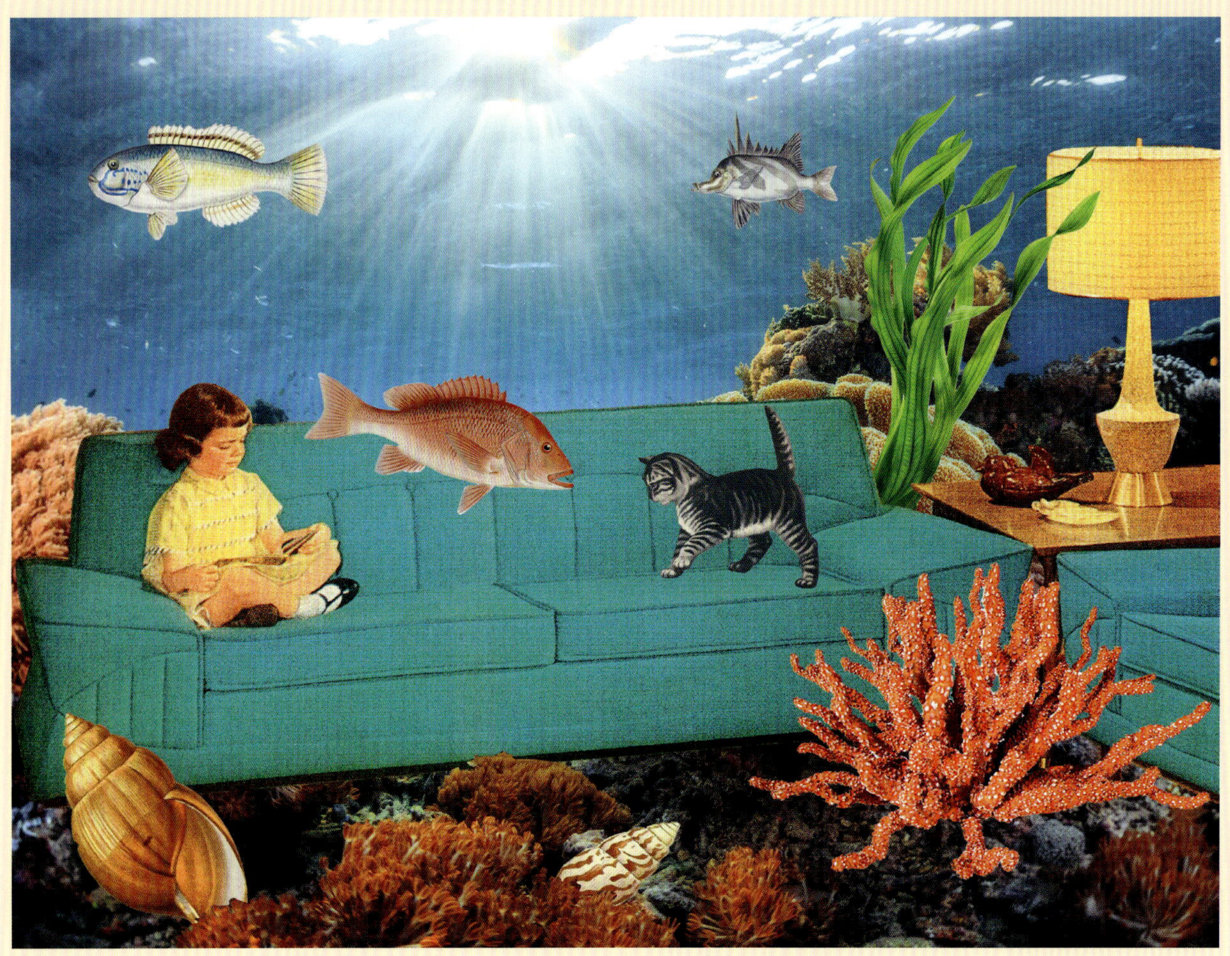

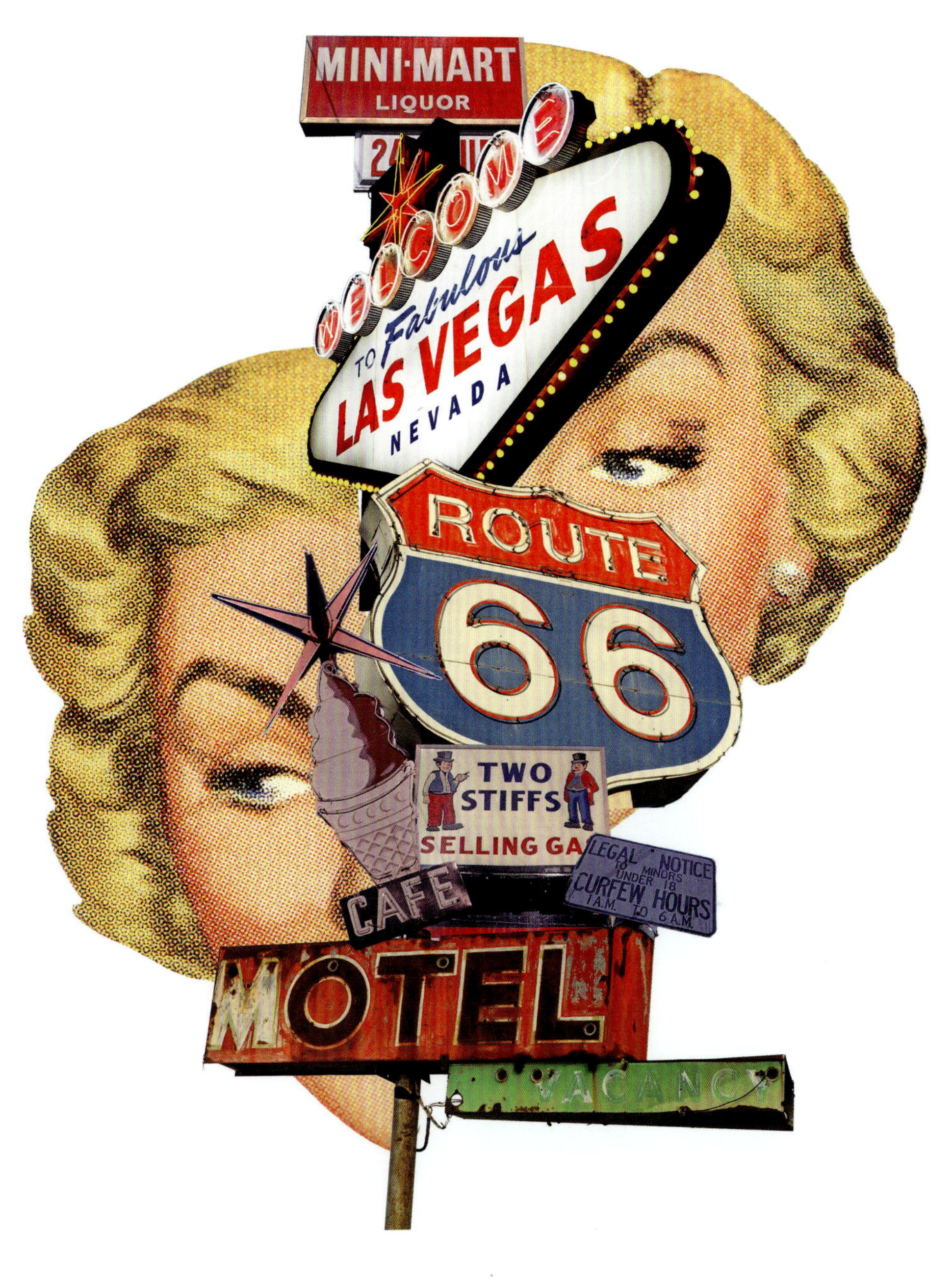

You don't always have to use the whole image.
Try cutting, tearing or isolating pieces to create a more abstract collage.

Swap out people for more interesting companions...

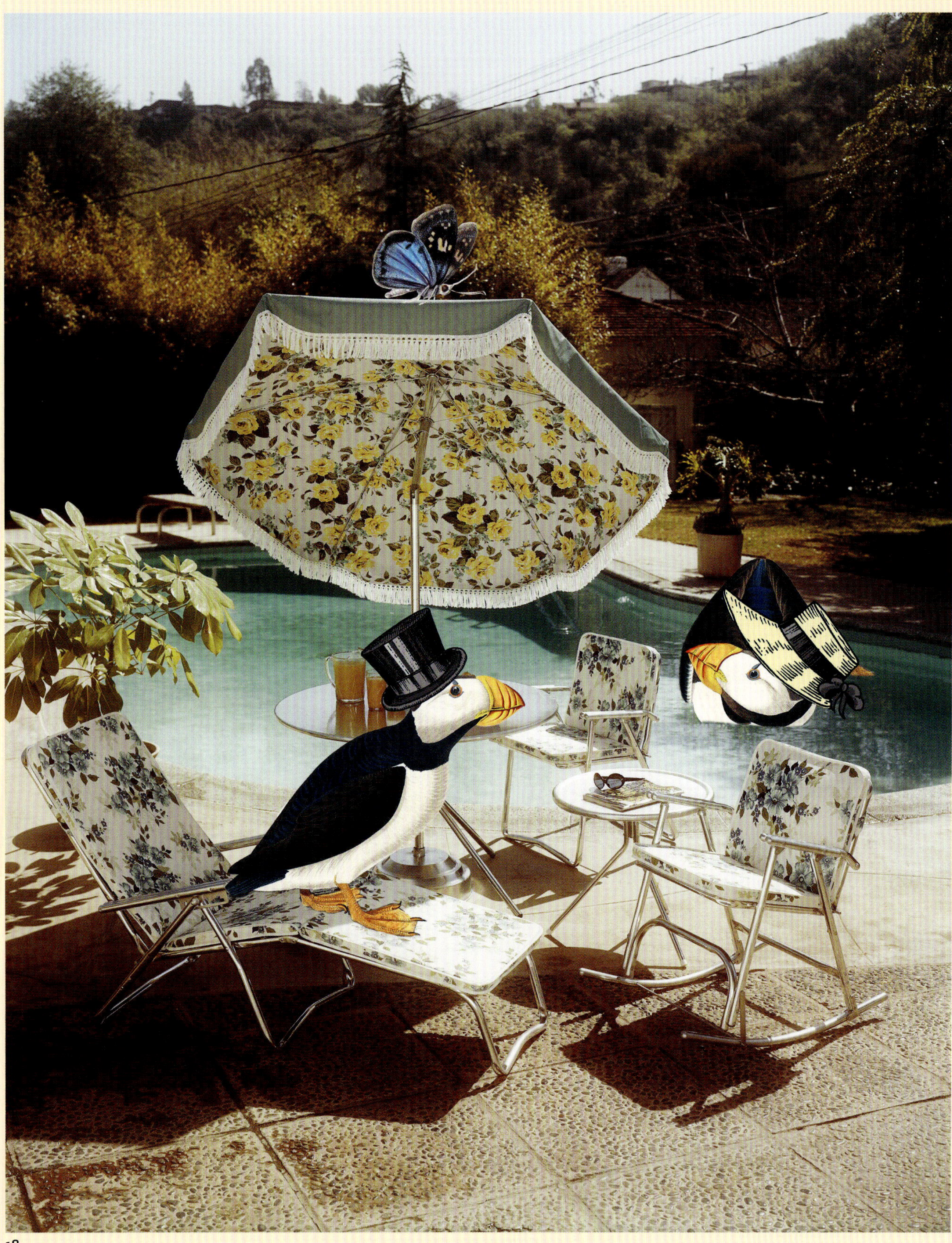

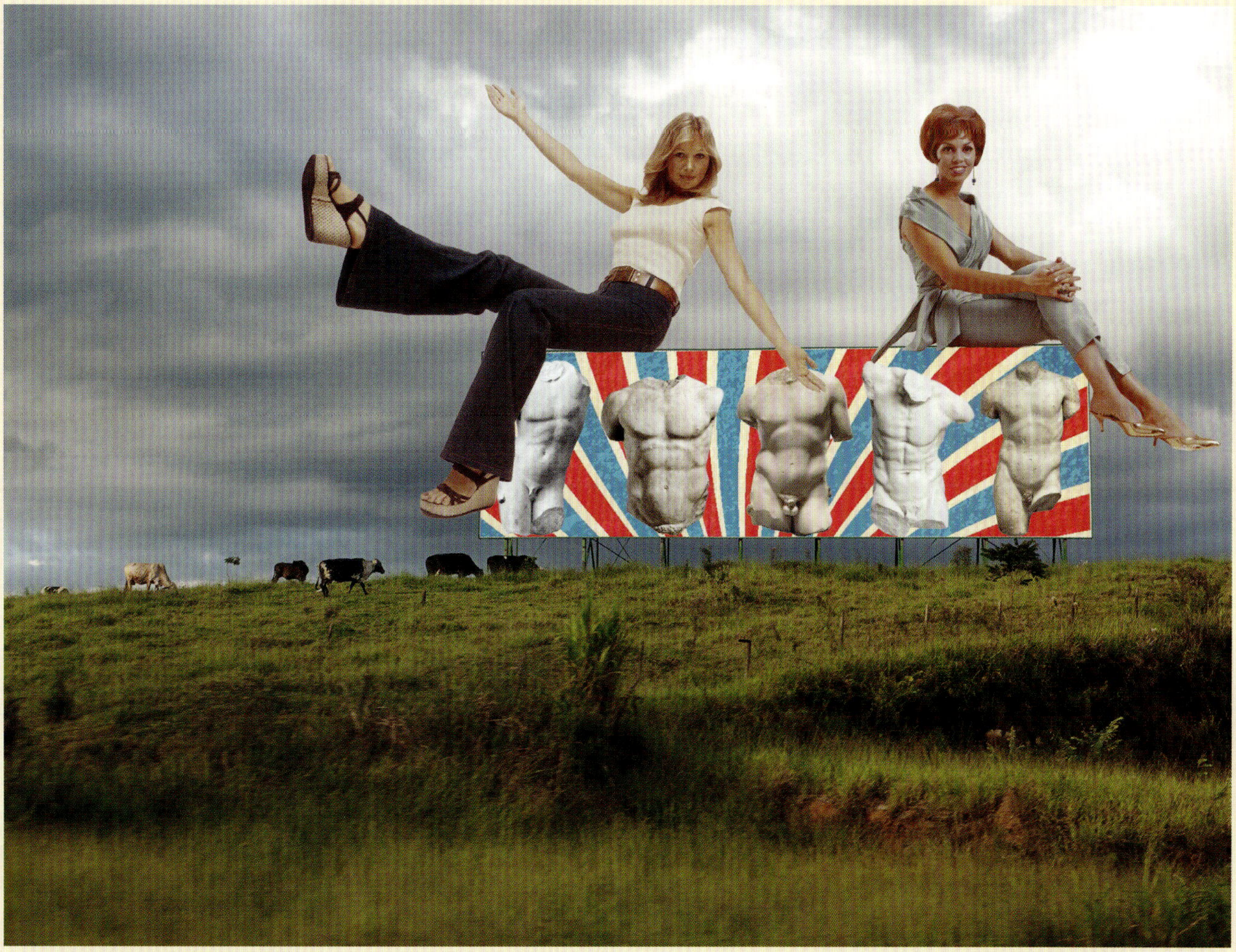

Scale is your best friend when making collages. It's my personal favourite design element to work with.

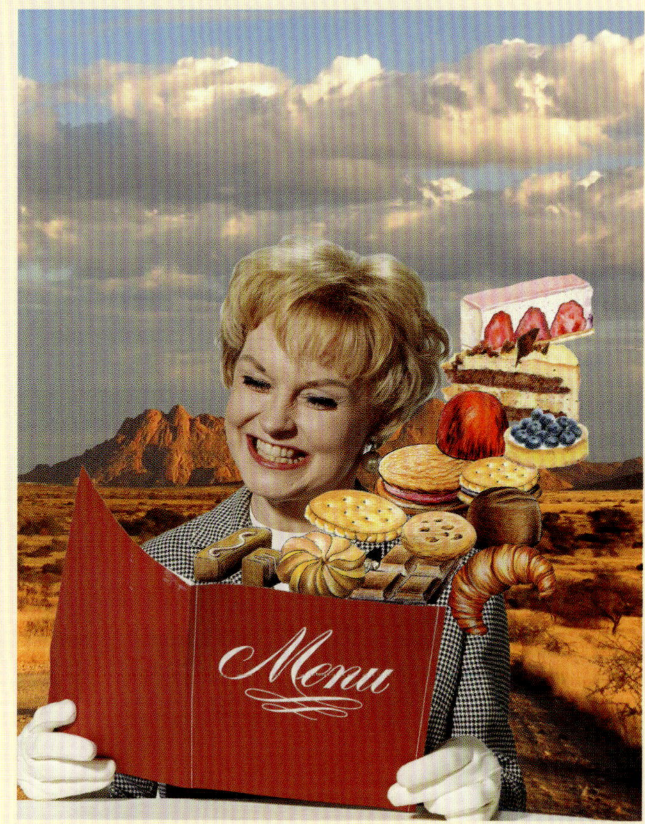

Use your passions to inspire your art. Love a sweet treat? Let's see a collage all about cookies, cakes, pastries and chocolates!

Nature

Flowers....23
Trees....27
Mushrooms....29
Fruit....31
Feathers....33
Birds....35
Butterflies....37
Animals....39
Cats....43
Sea Life....45
Fish....47

People & Domestic Life

People....49
Food....67
Tea Cups....69
Hats....71
Sunglasses....73
Clocks....75
Cards & Games....77
Frames....79
TVs....81
Chairs....83
Furniture & Appliances....87

Transport & Technology

Cars....91
Planes, Boats & Trains....93
Hot Air Balloons....95
Space & Robots....97
Old-fashioned....99

Urban Life

Landmarks....101
Old Architecture....103
Buildings....105

Repeats

Gemstones....107
Speech Bubbles....109
Stars....111
Flowers....113

Backgrounds

Countryside....115
Mountains....119
Street scene....123
Domestic scene: House....125
Domestic scene: Pool....127
Domestic scene: Office Desk....129
Domestic scene: Christmas....131
Underwater....133
Space....135
Flower....137
Psychedelic....139
Figures....141

1,000 Images to Cut Out & Collage

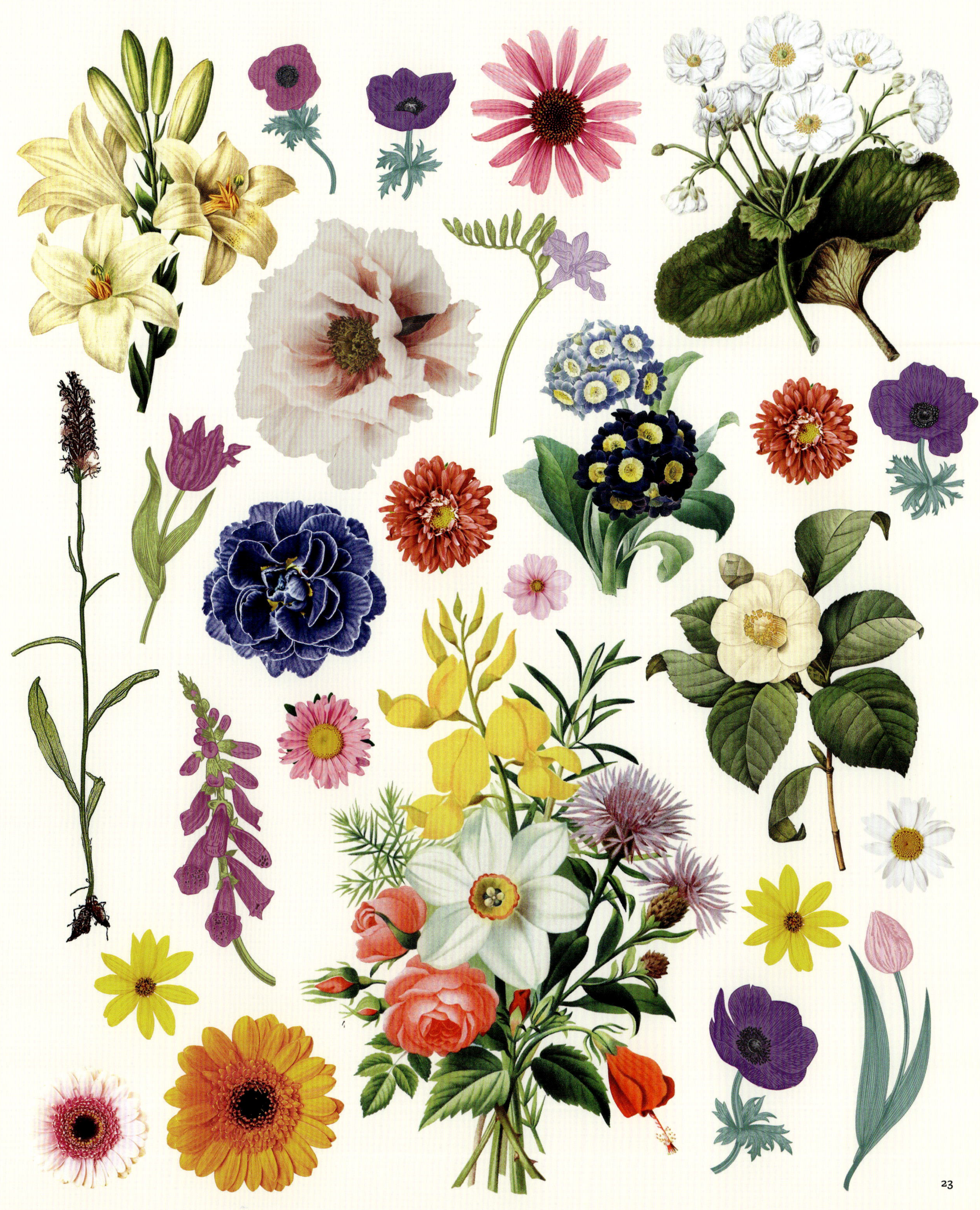

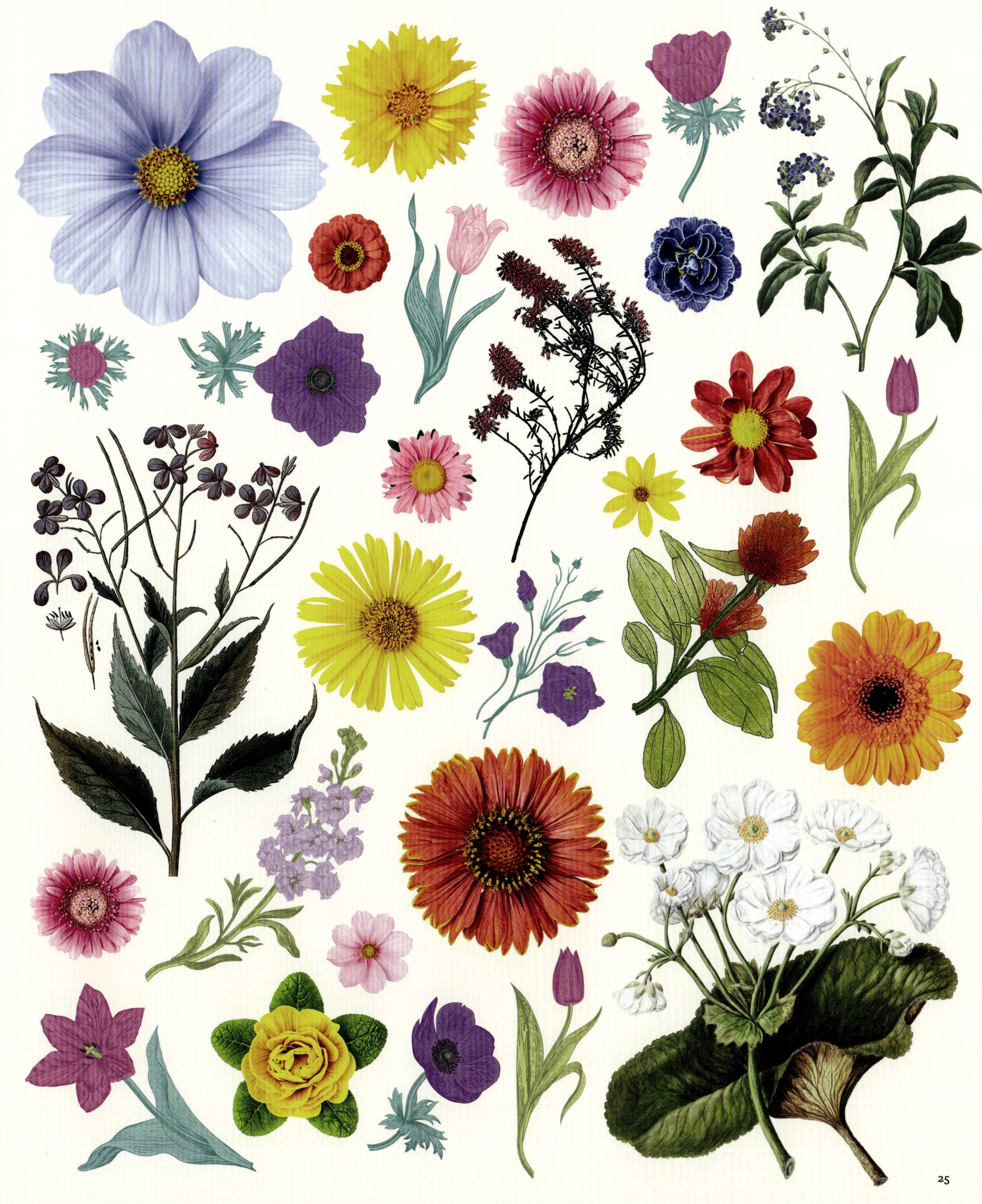

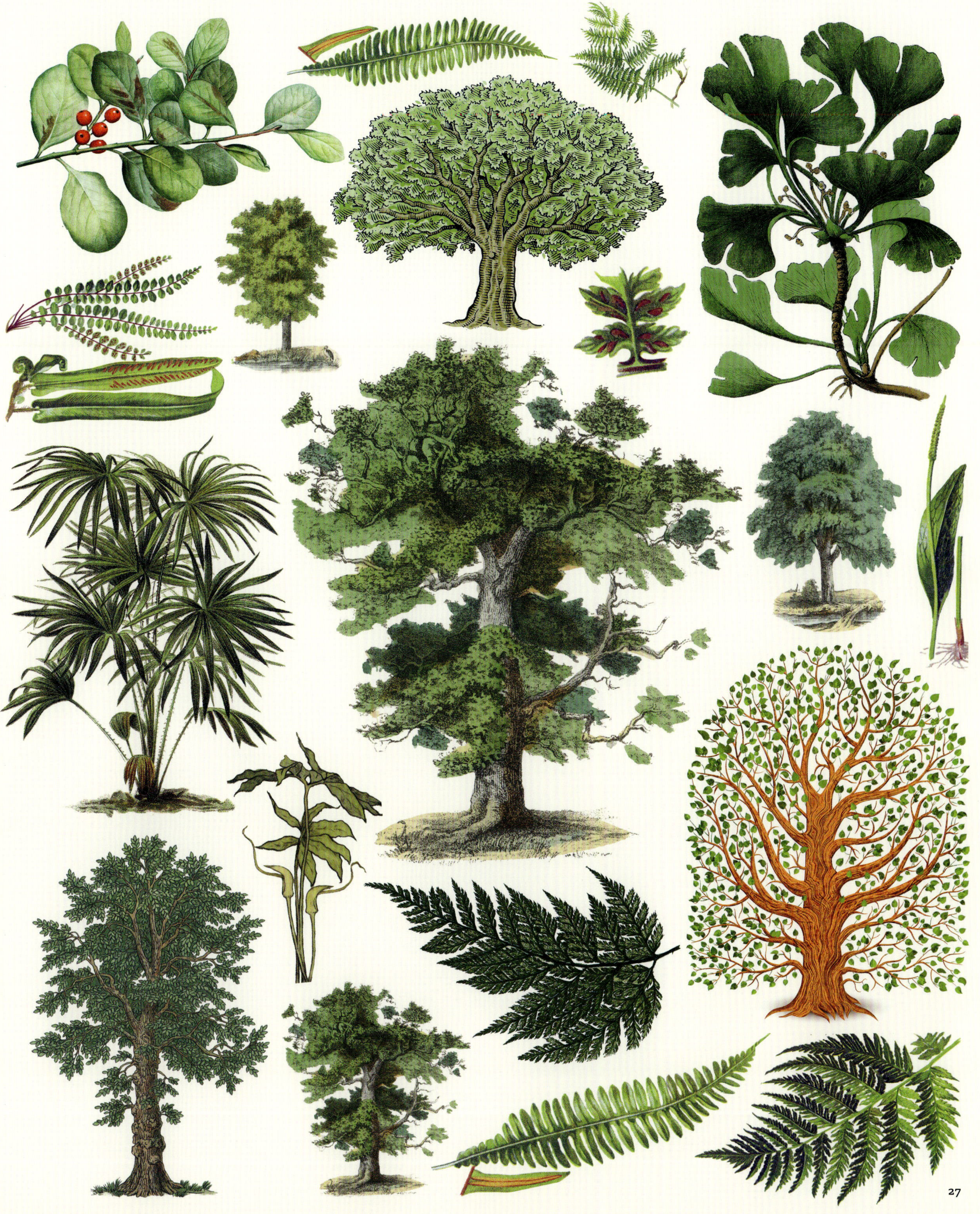

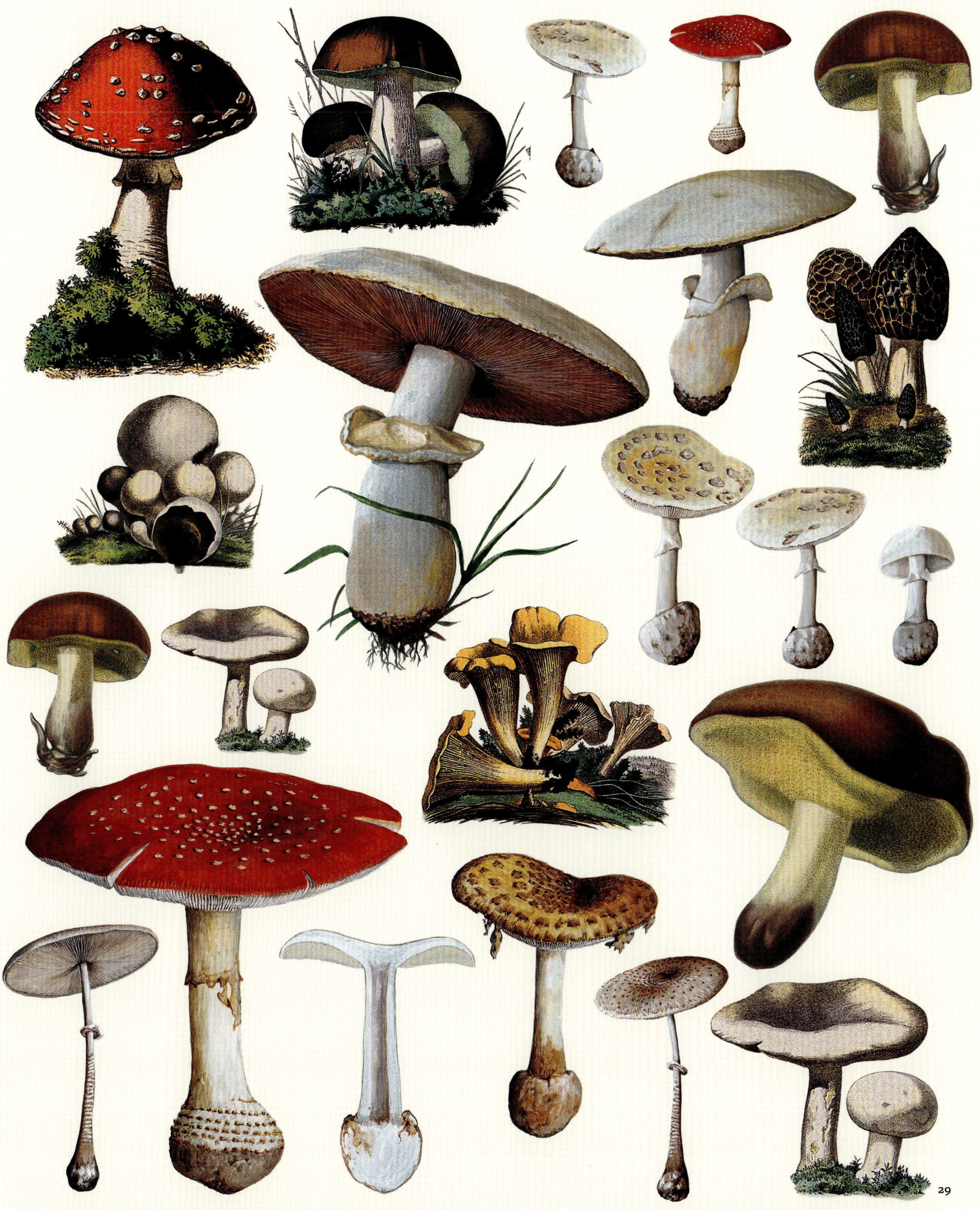

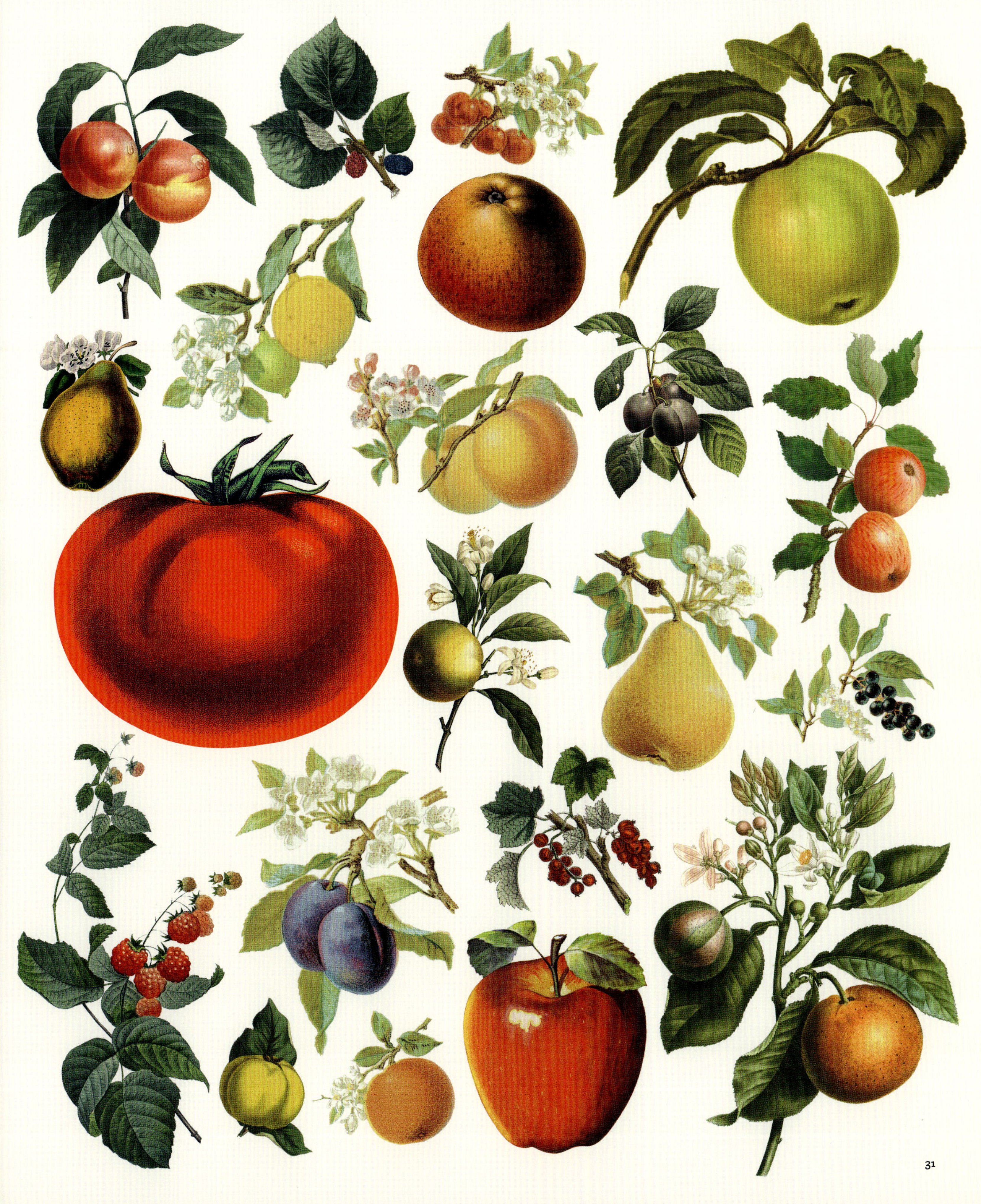

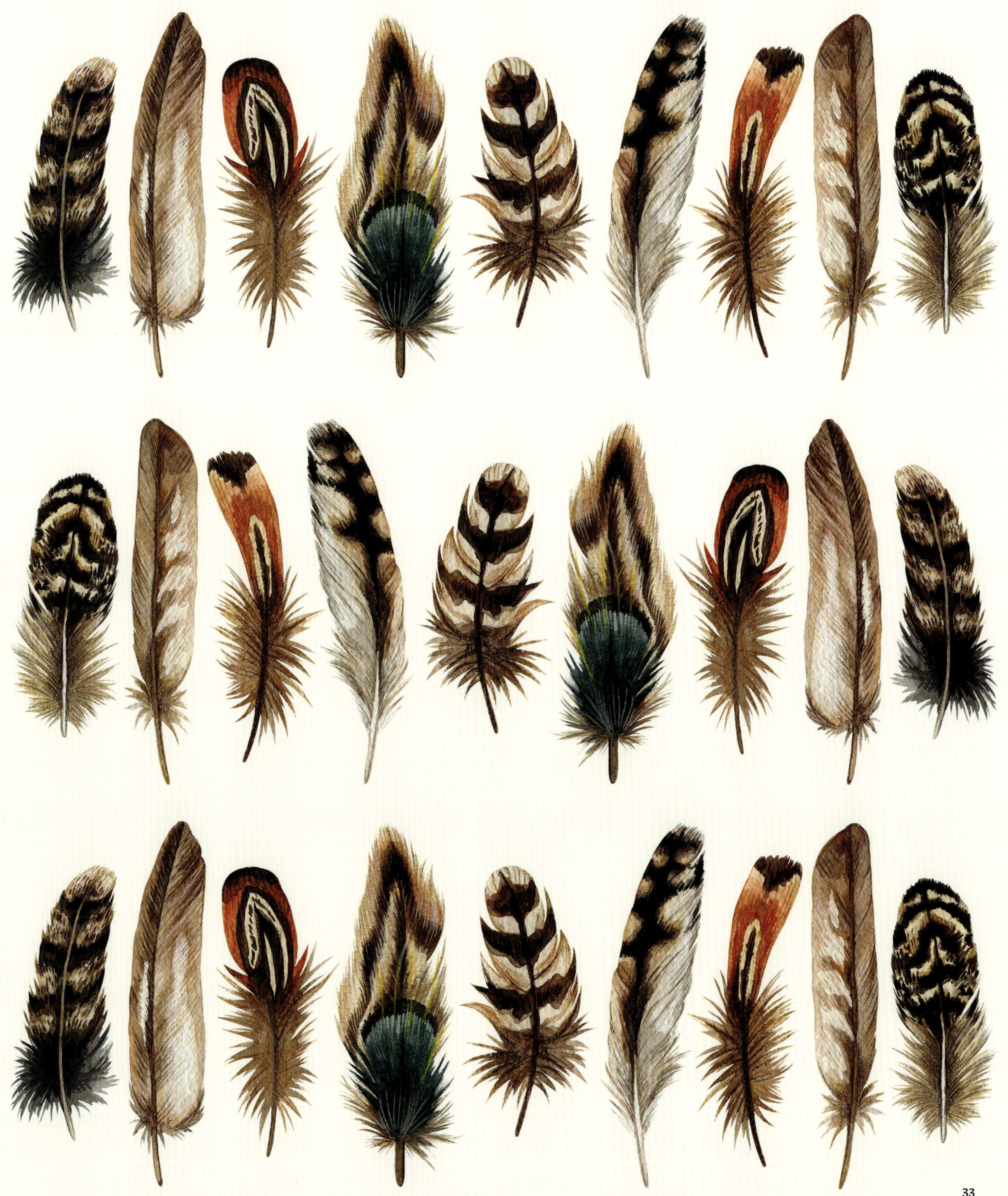

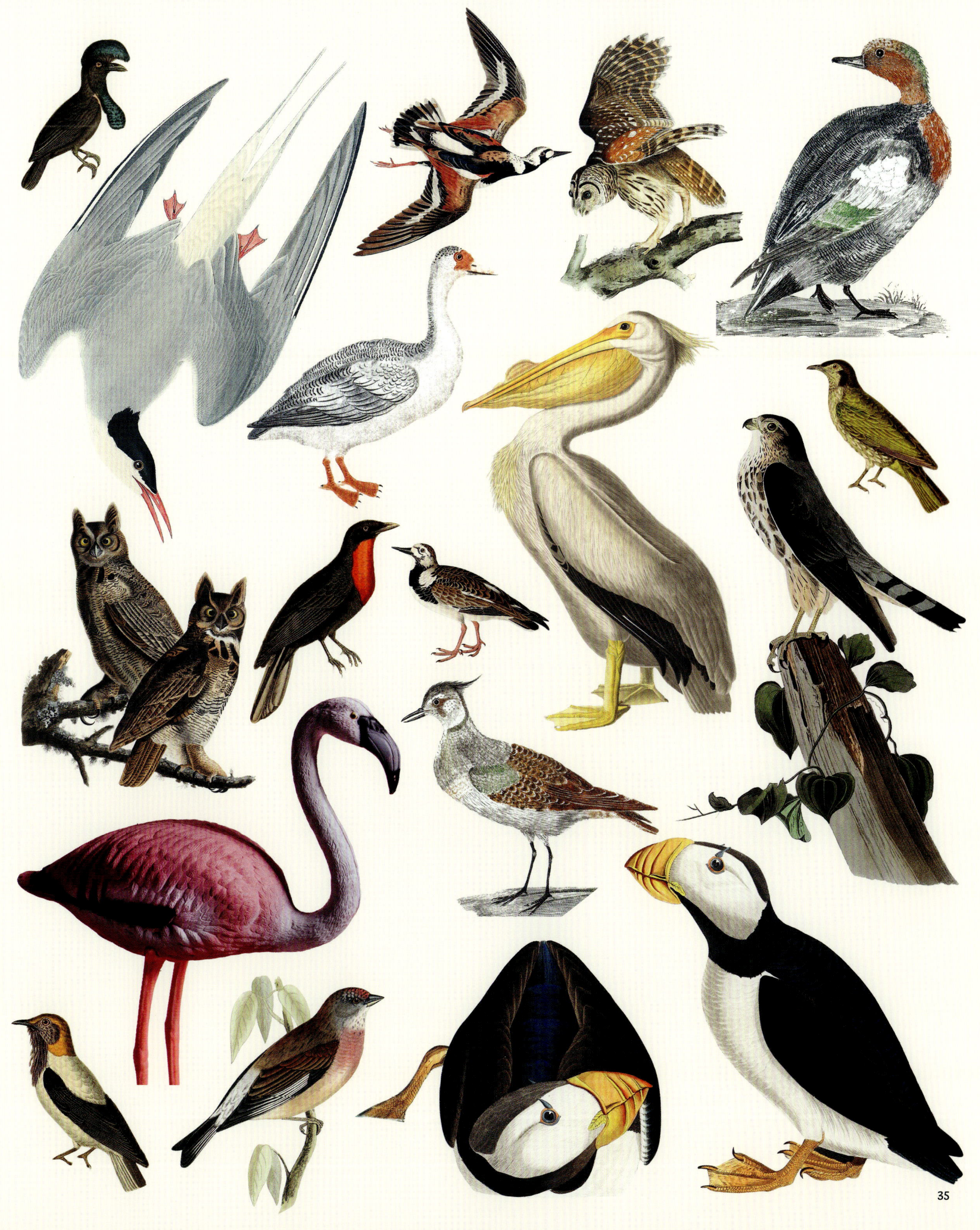

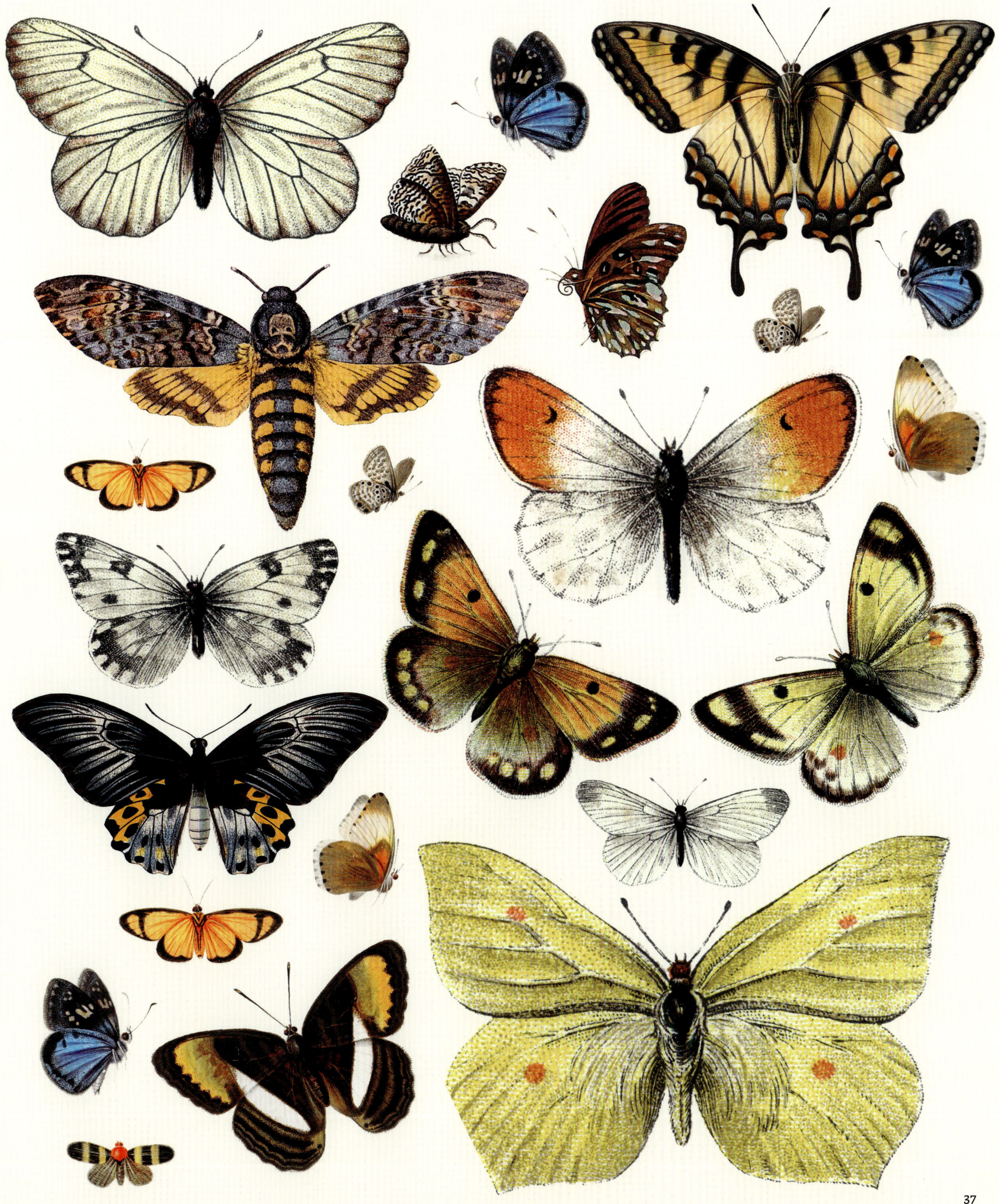

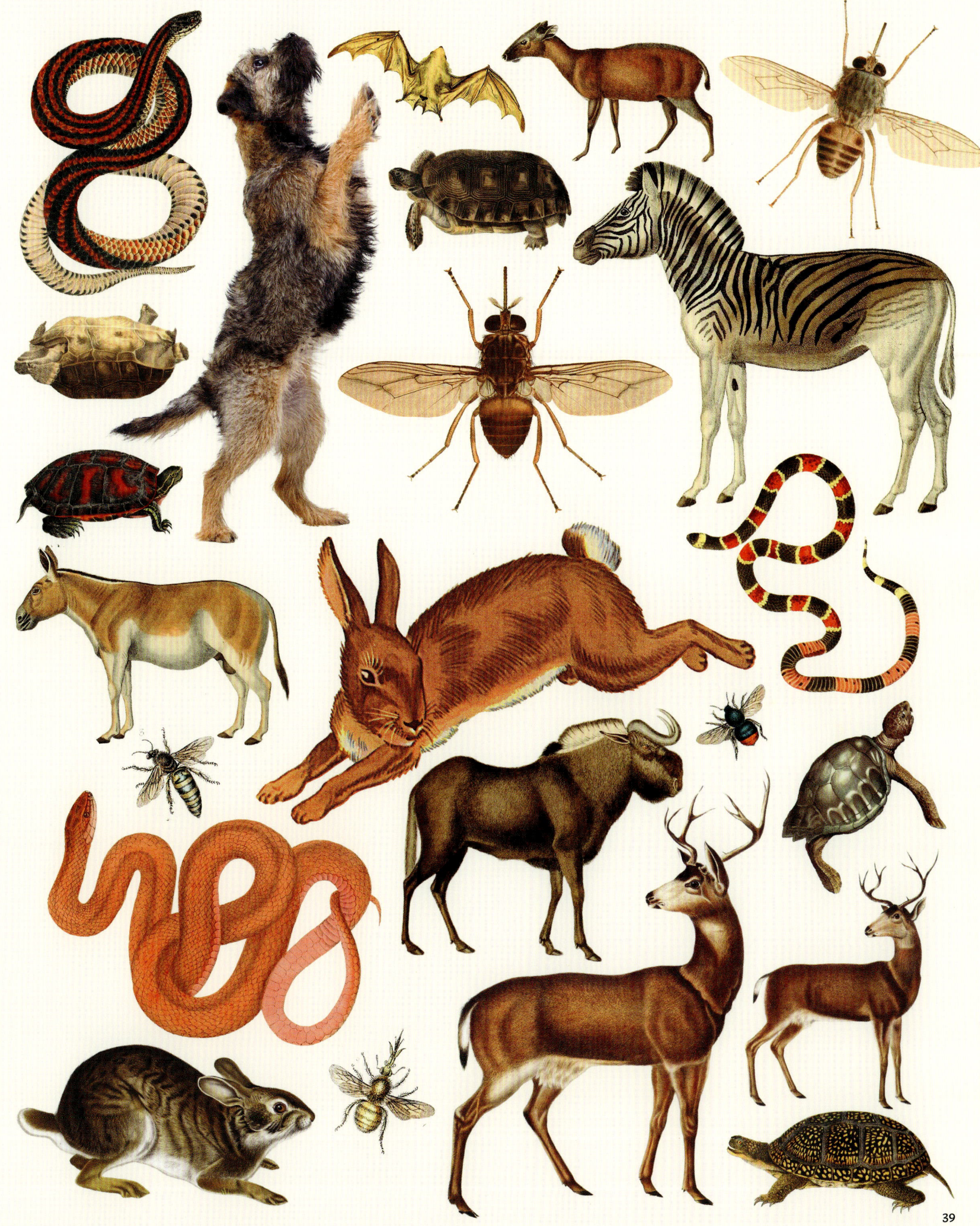

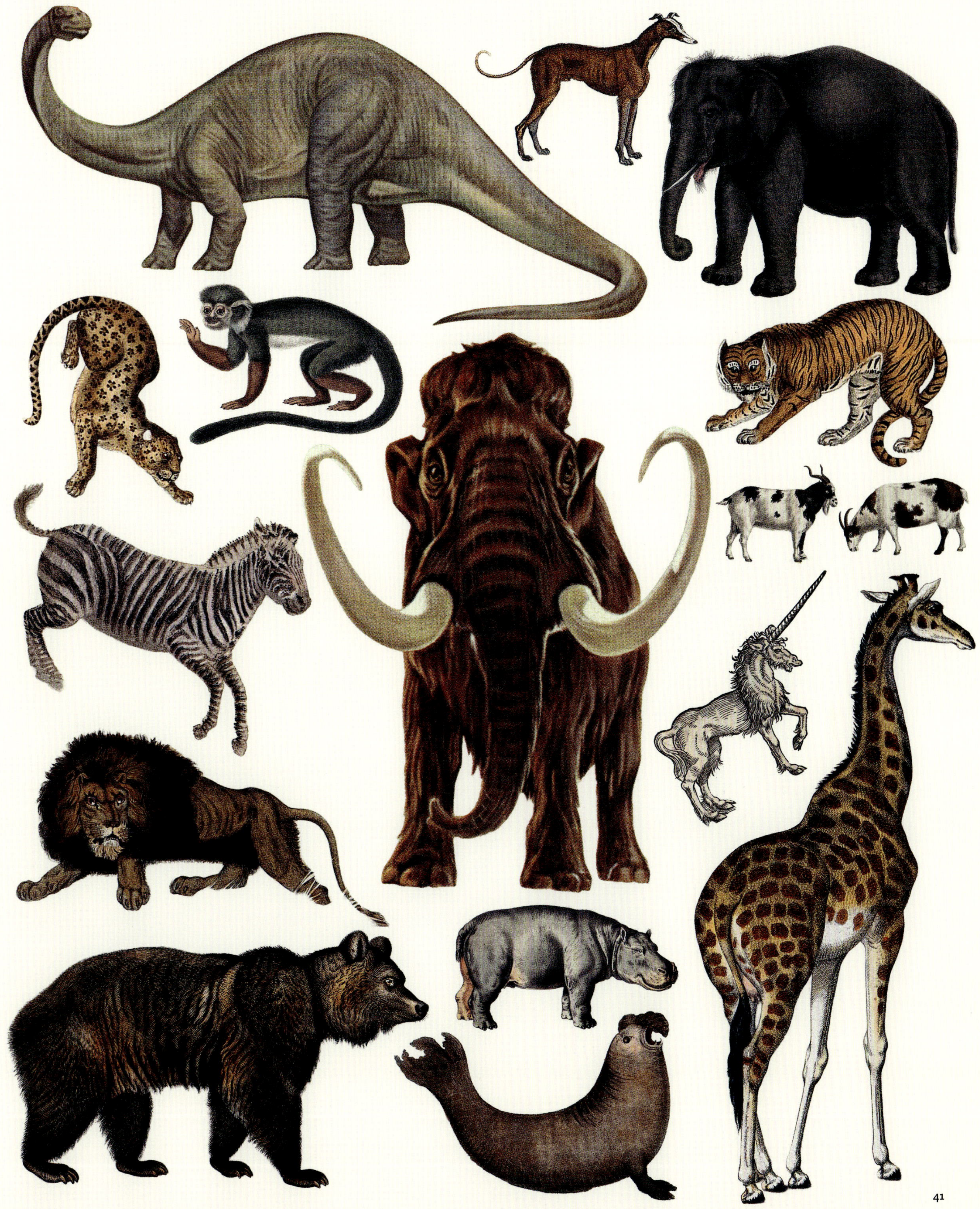

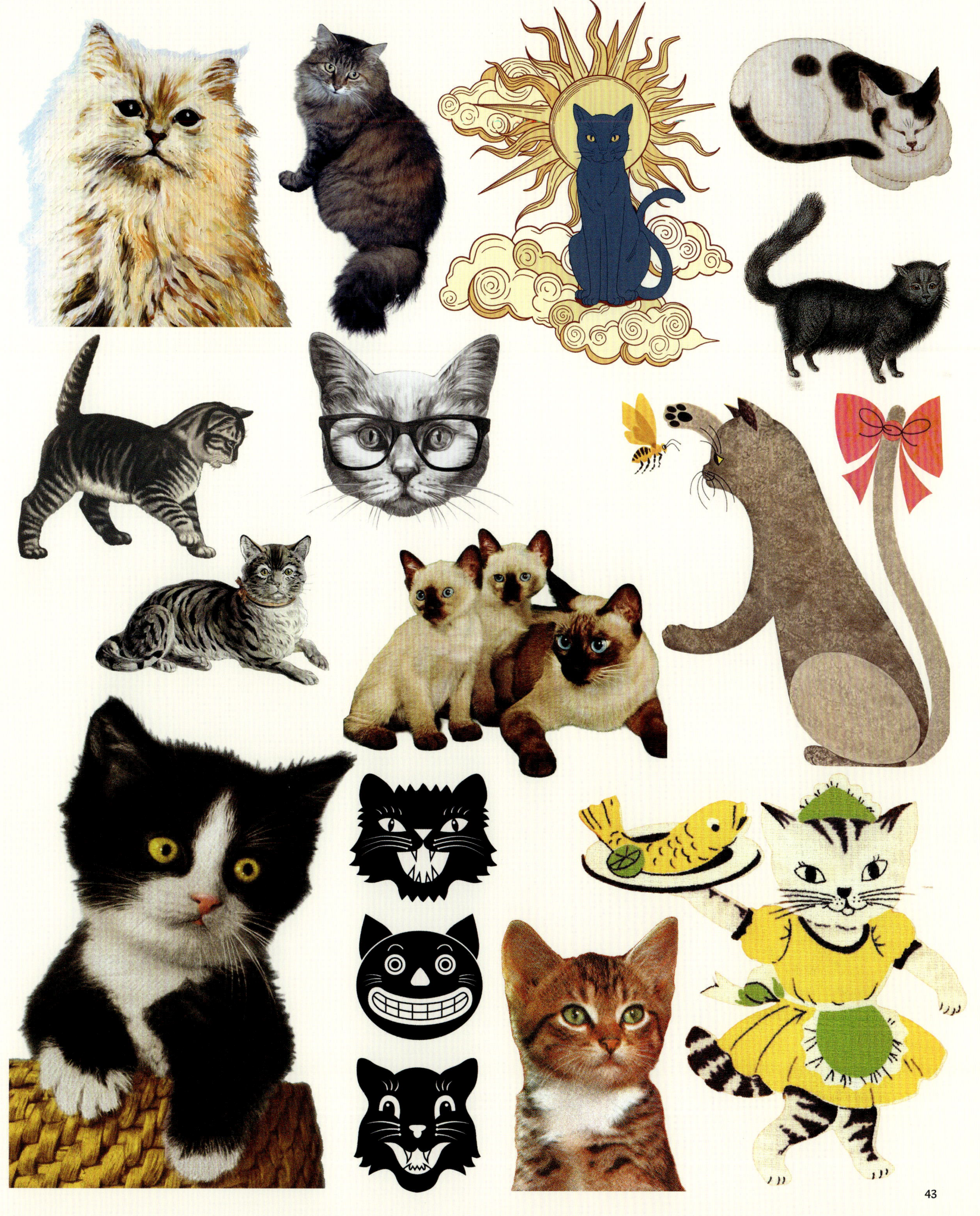

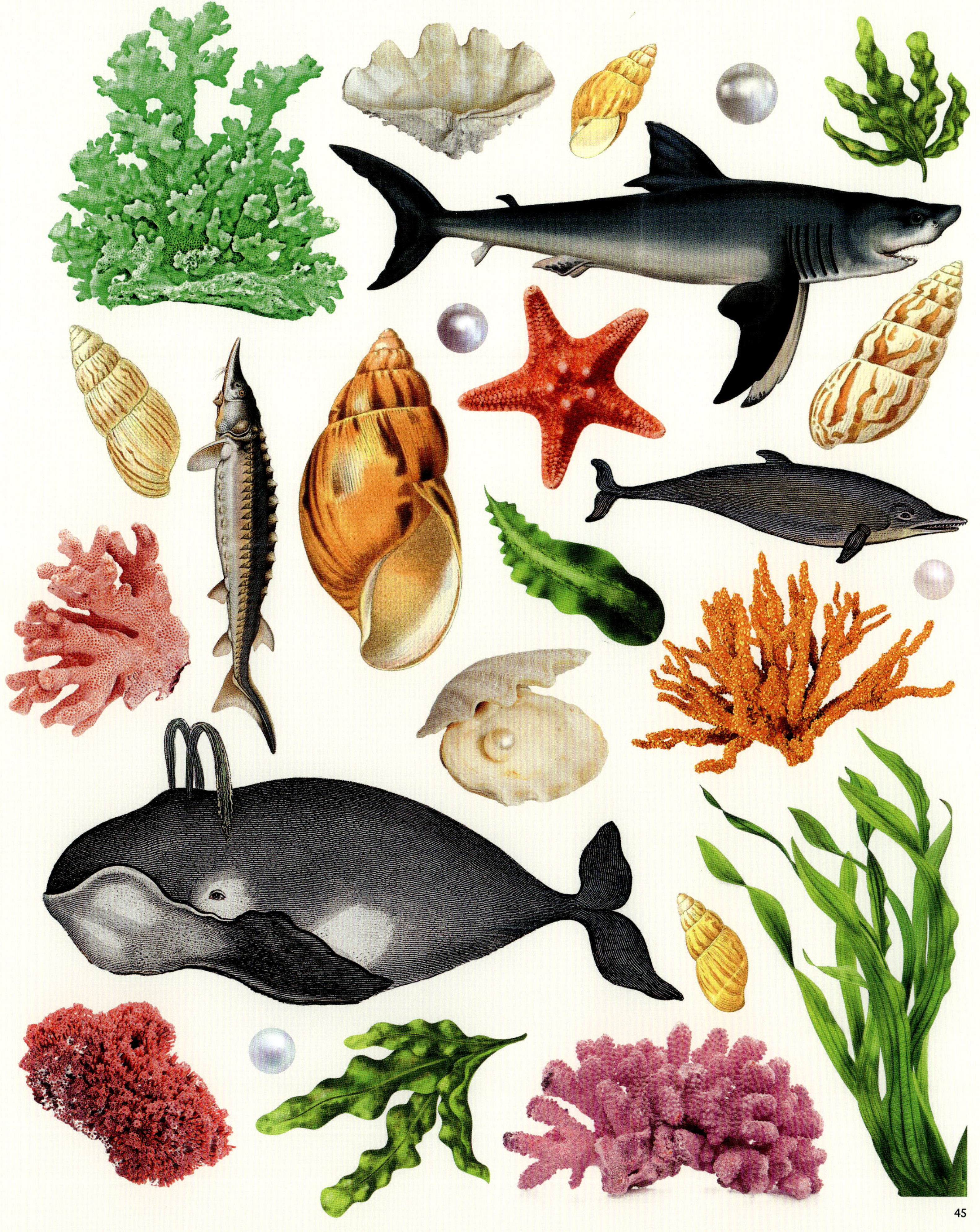

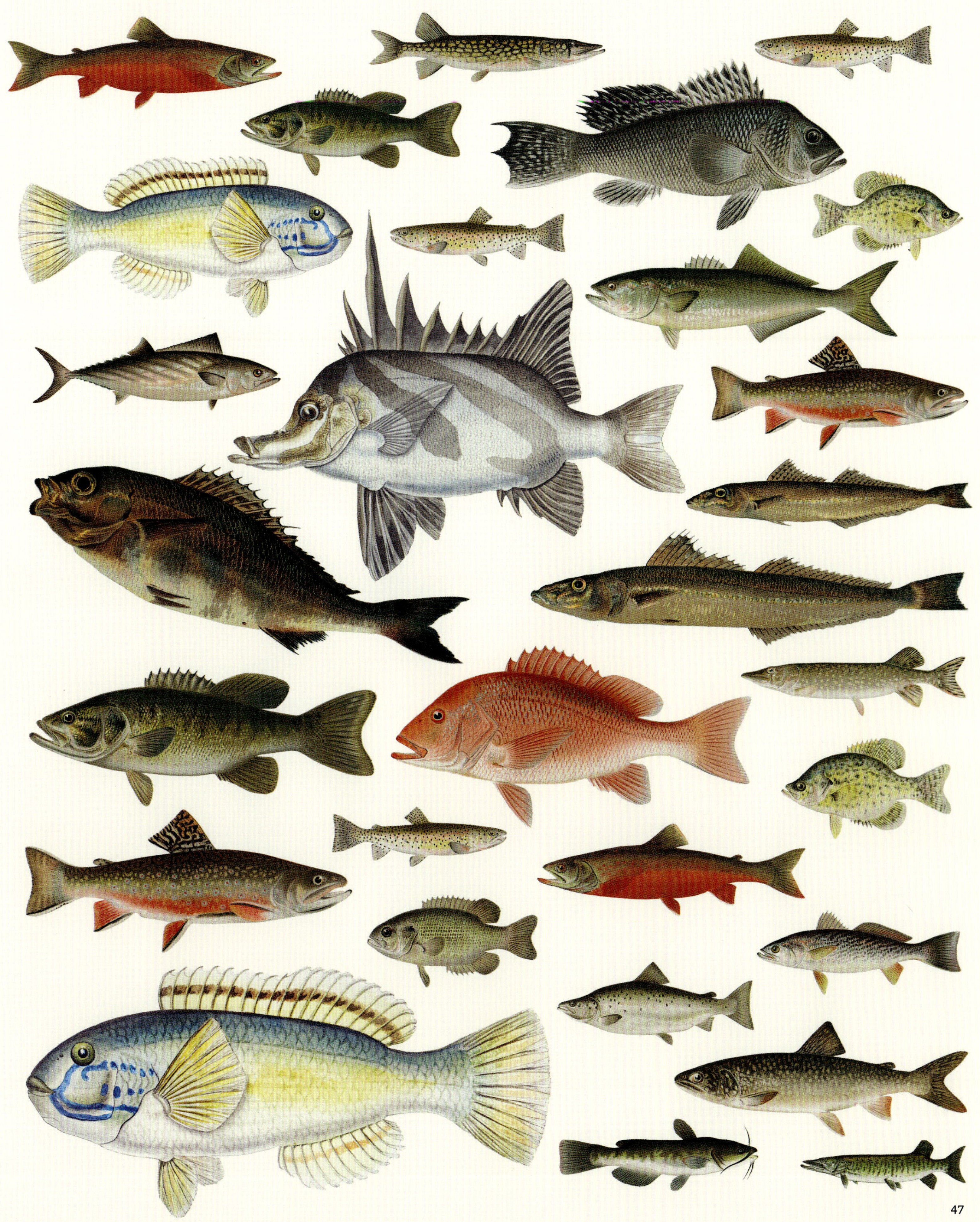

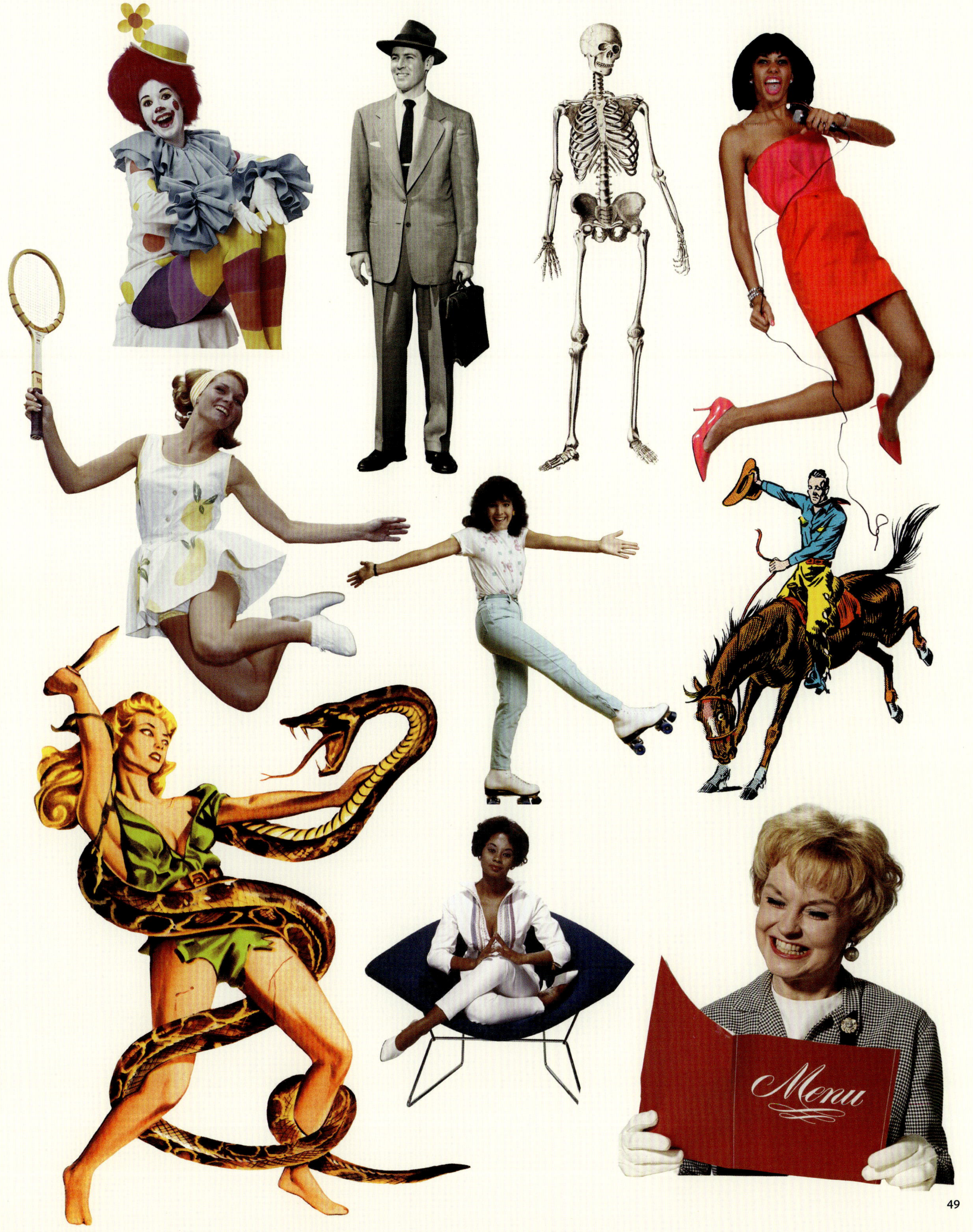
Menu

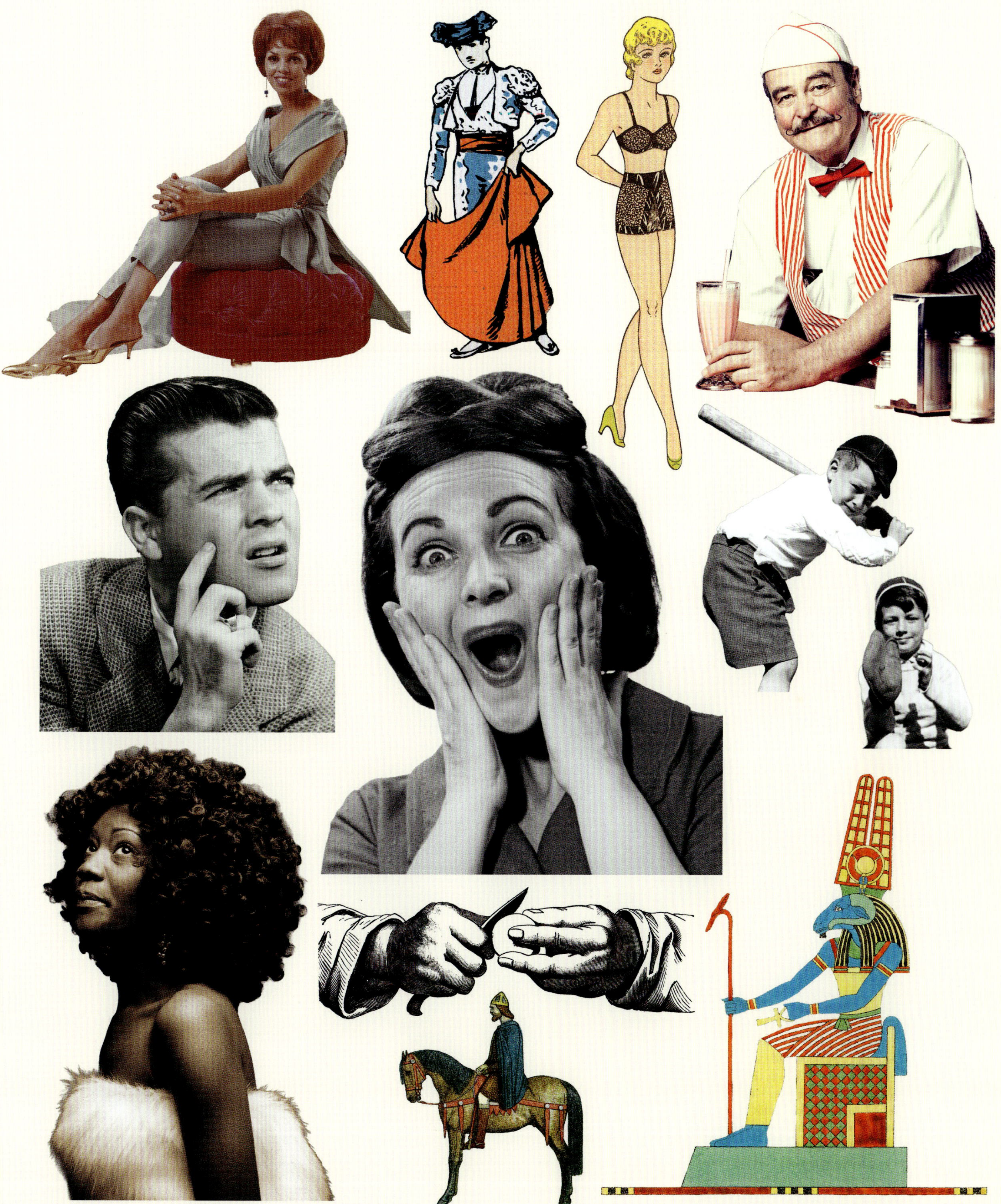

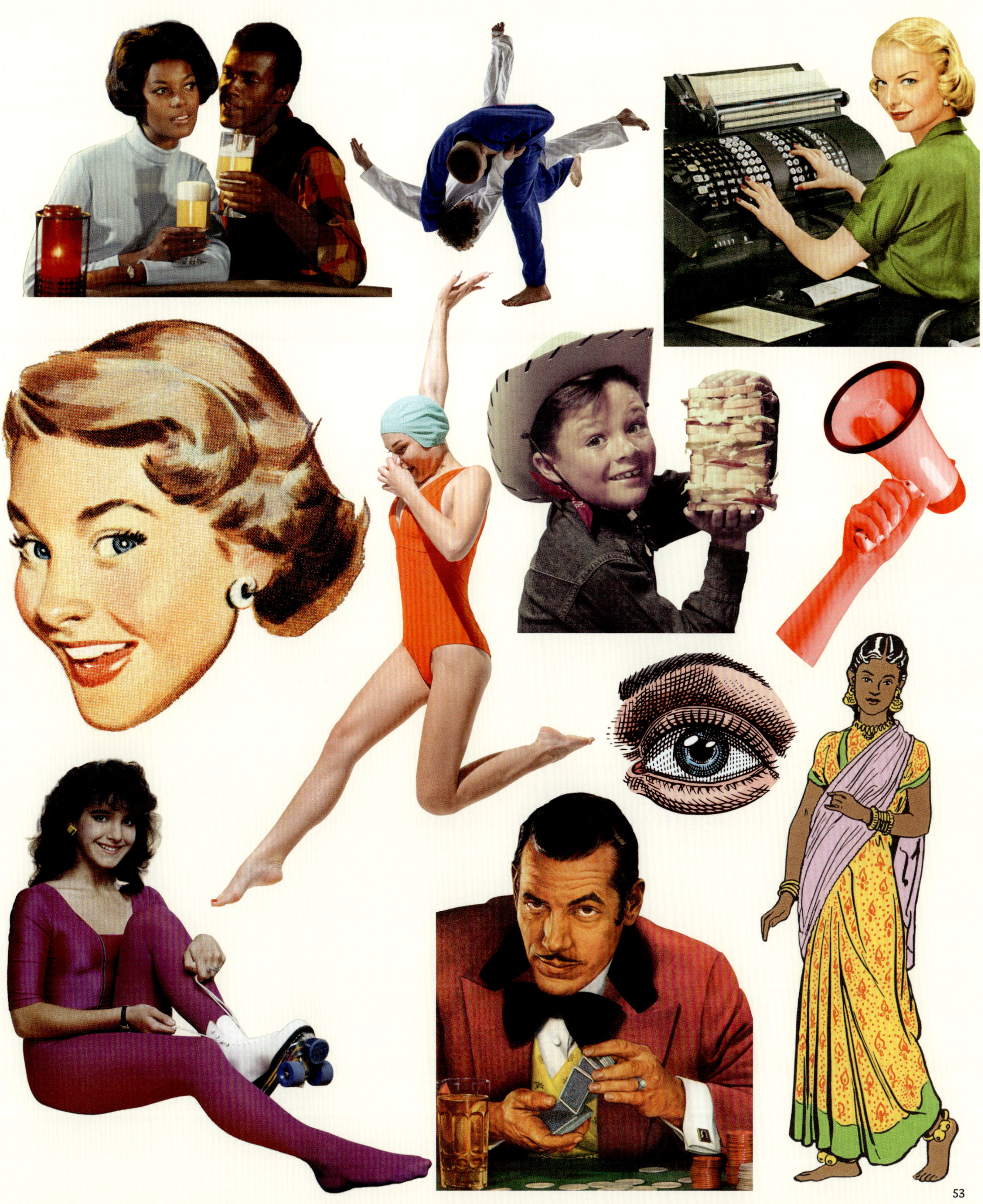

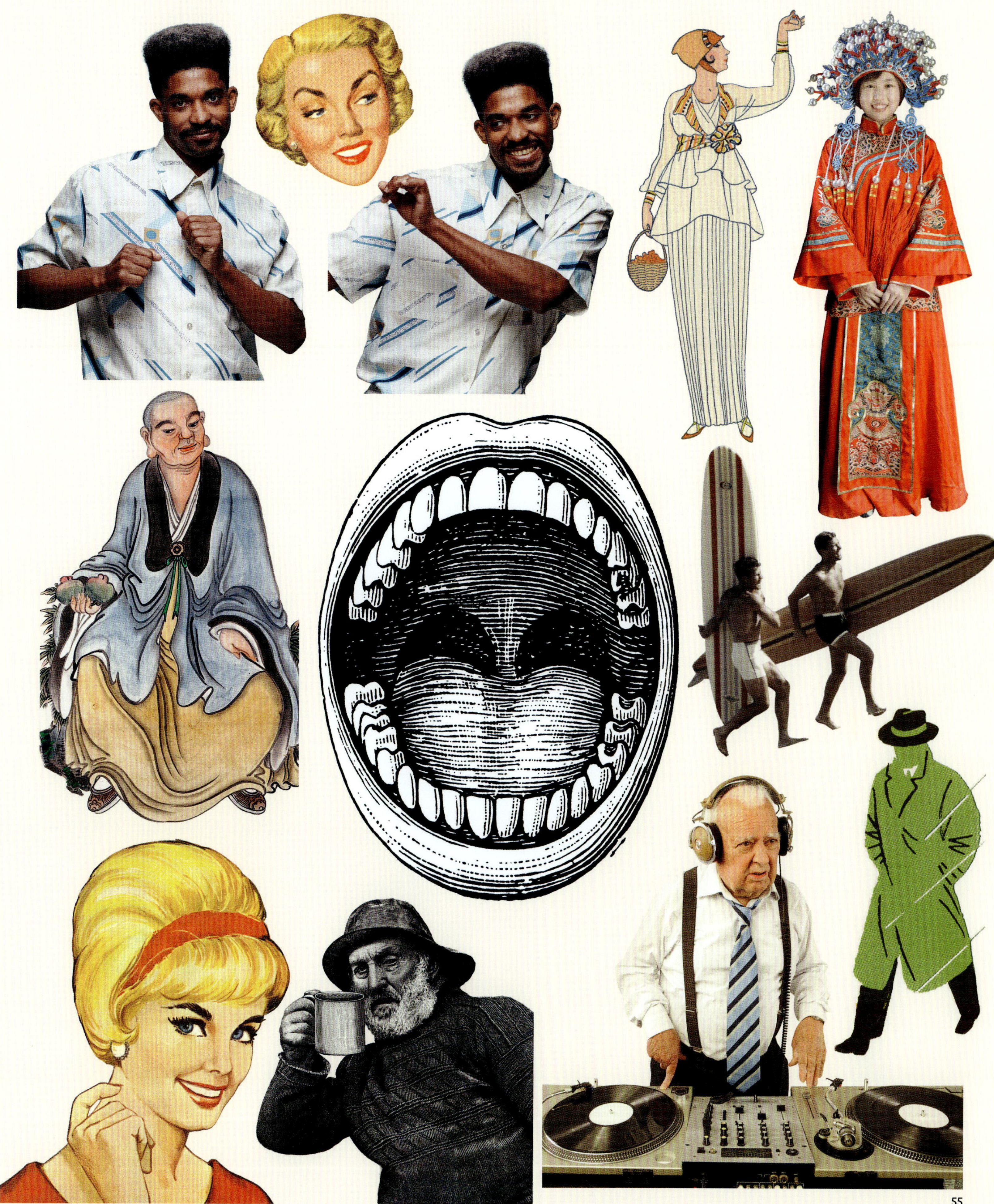

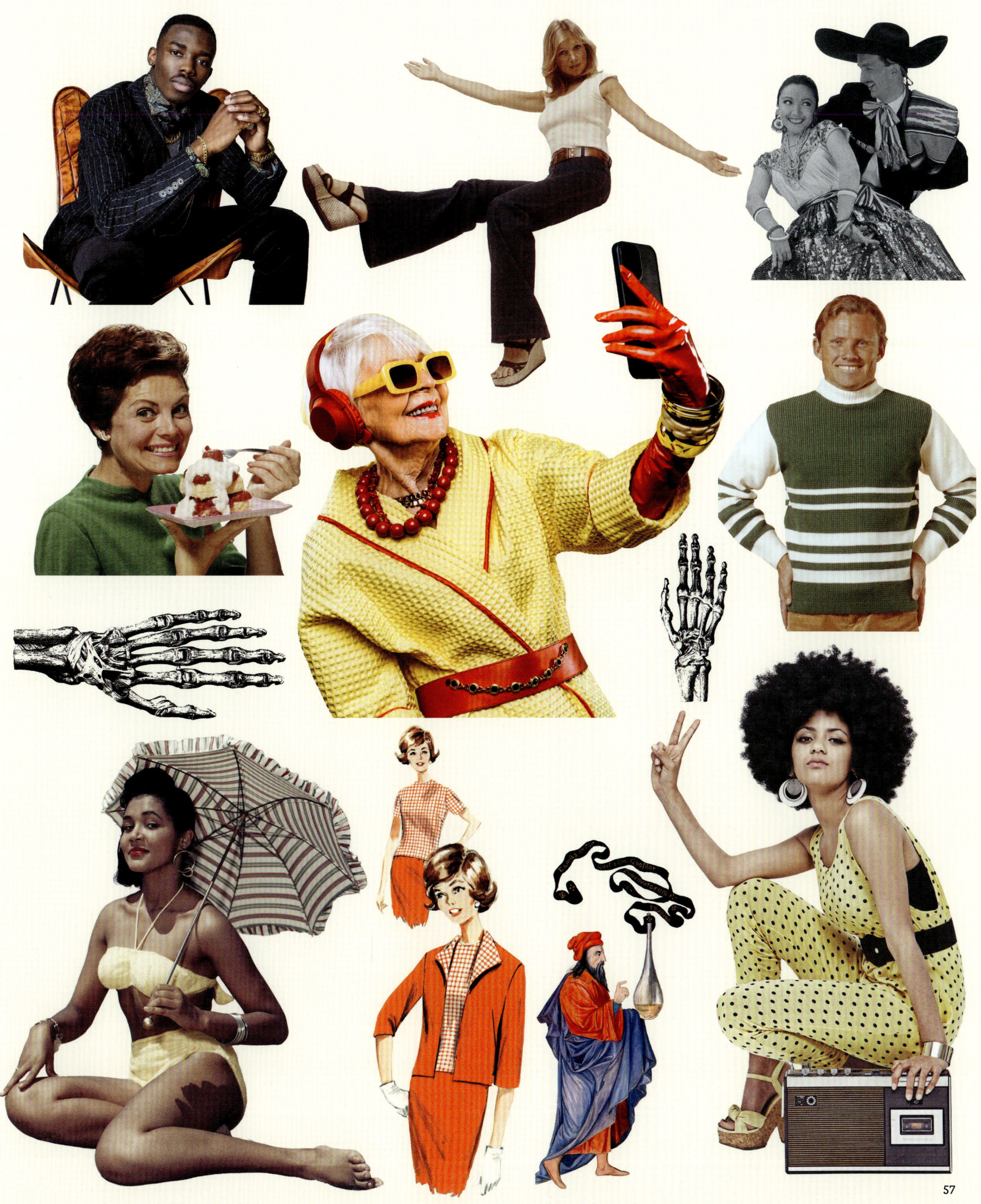
Eamus
Quatuor
Elementorum

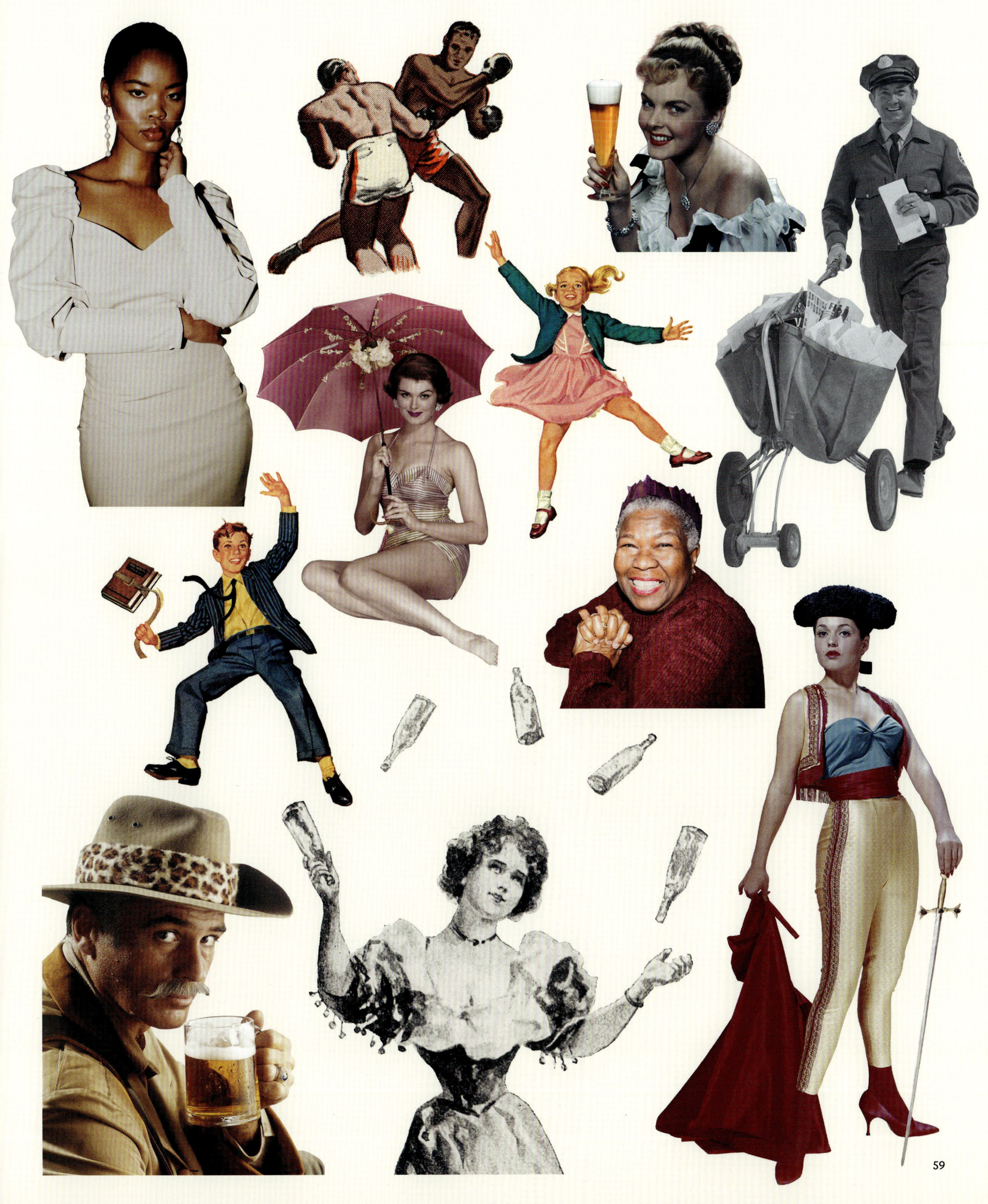

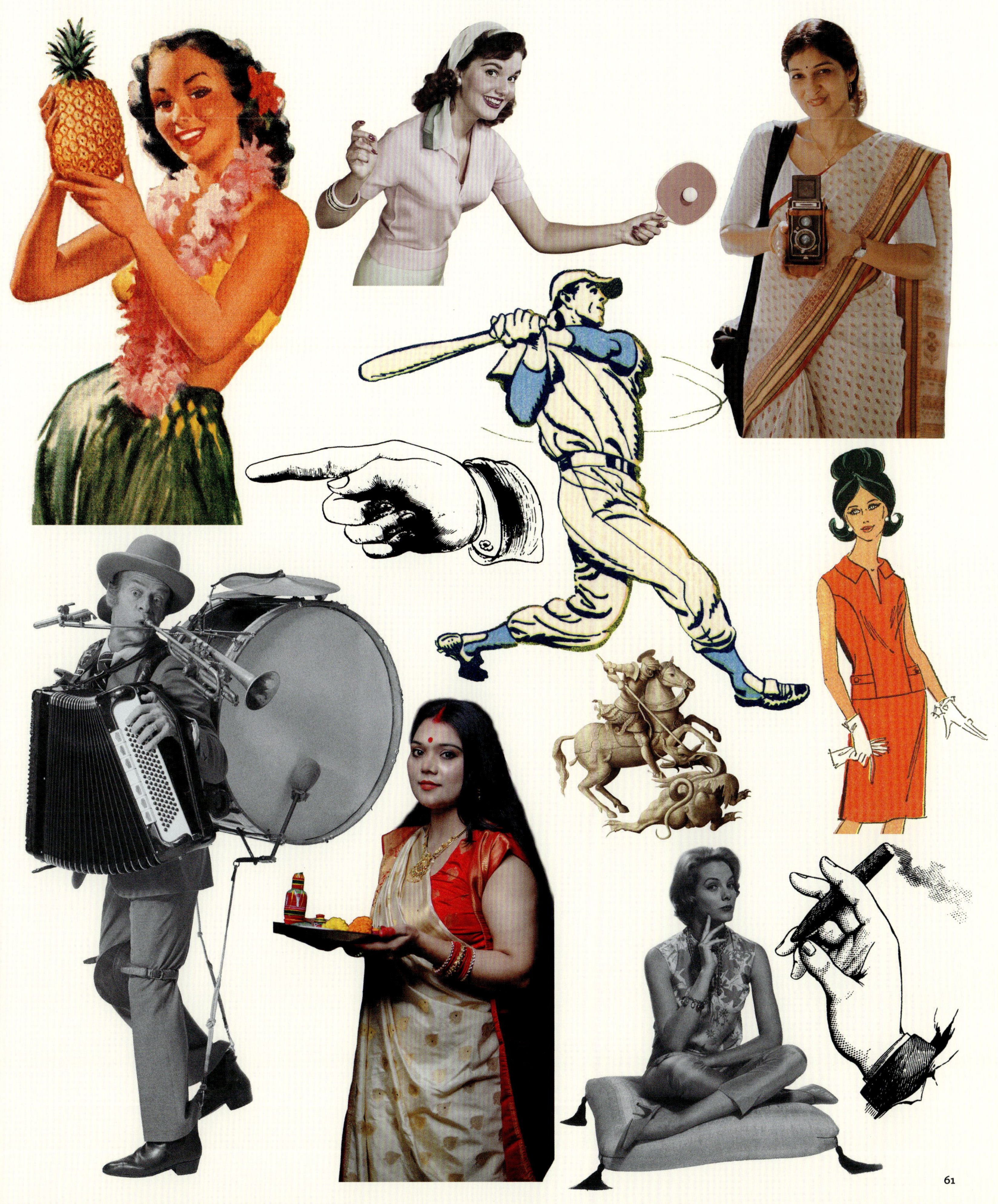

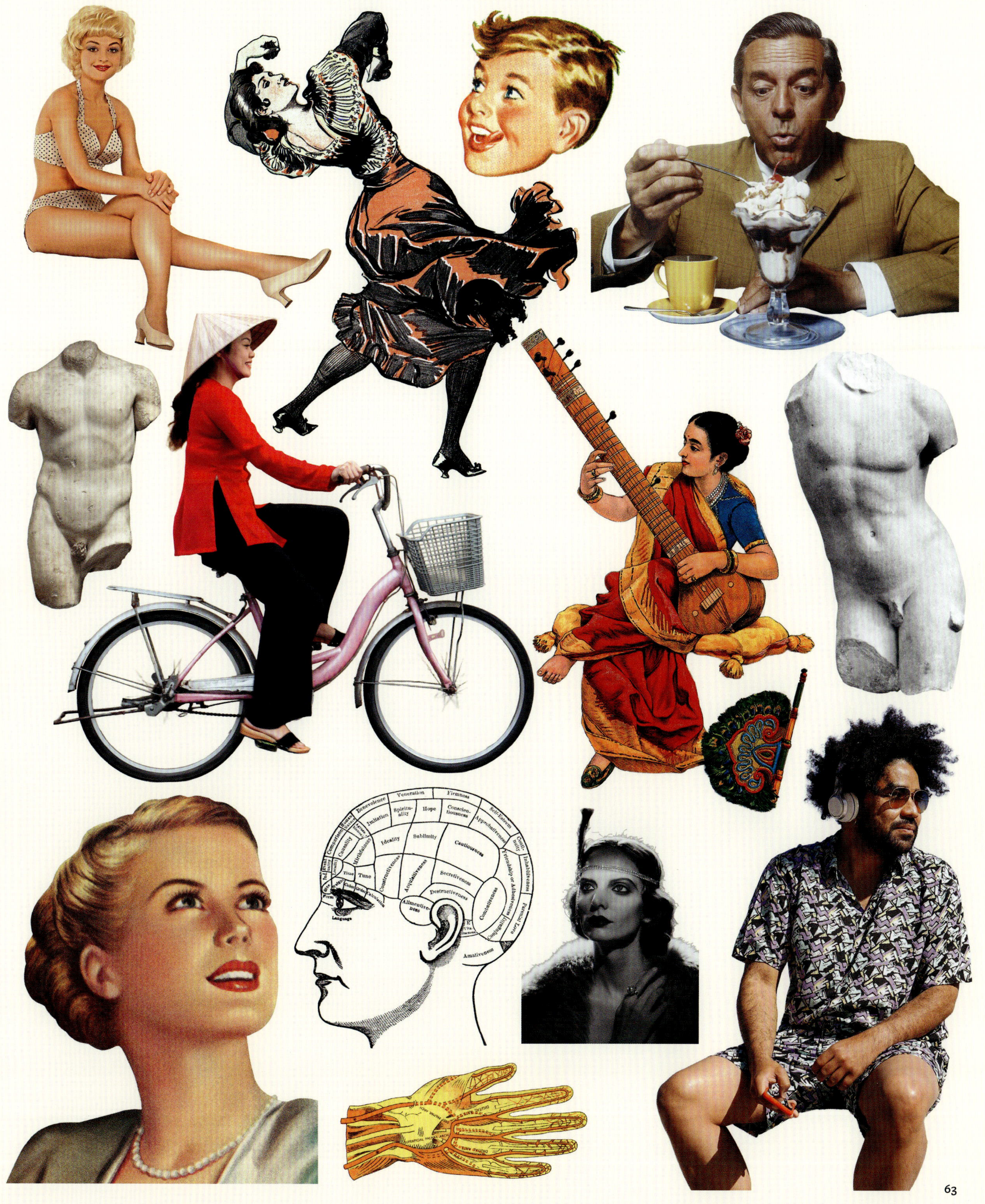
Veneration
Firmness
Benevolence
Spiritu-
ality
Hope
Conscien-
tiousness
Self-Esteem
Human
Nature
Imitation
Approbativeness
Comparison
Causality
Ideality
Sublimity
Conti-
nuity
Cautiousness
Mirthfulness
Friendship or Adhesiveness
Inhabitiveness
Event-
uality
Locality
Time
Tune
Constructiveness
Acquisitiveness
Secretiveness
Size
Color
Order
Calculation
Destructiveness
Form
Alimentive-
ness
Combativeness
Parental Love
Language
Conjugality
Amativeness

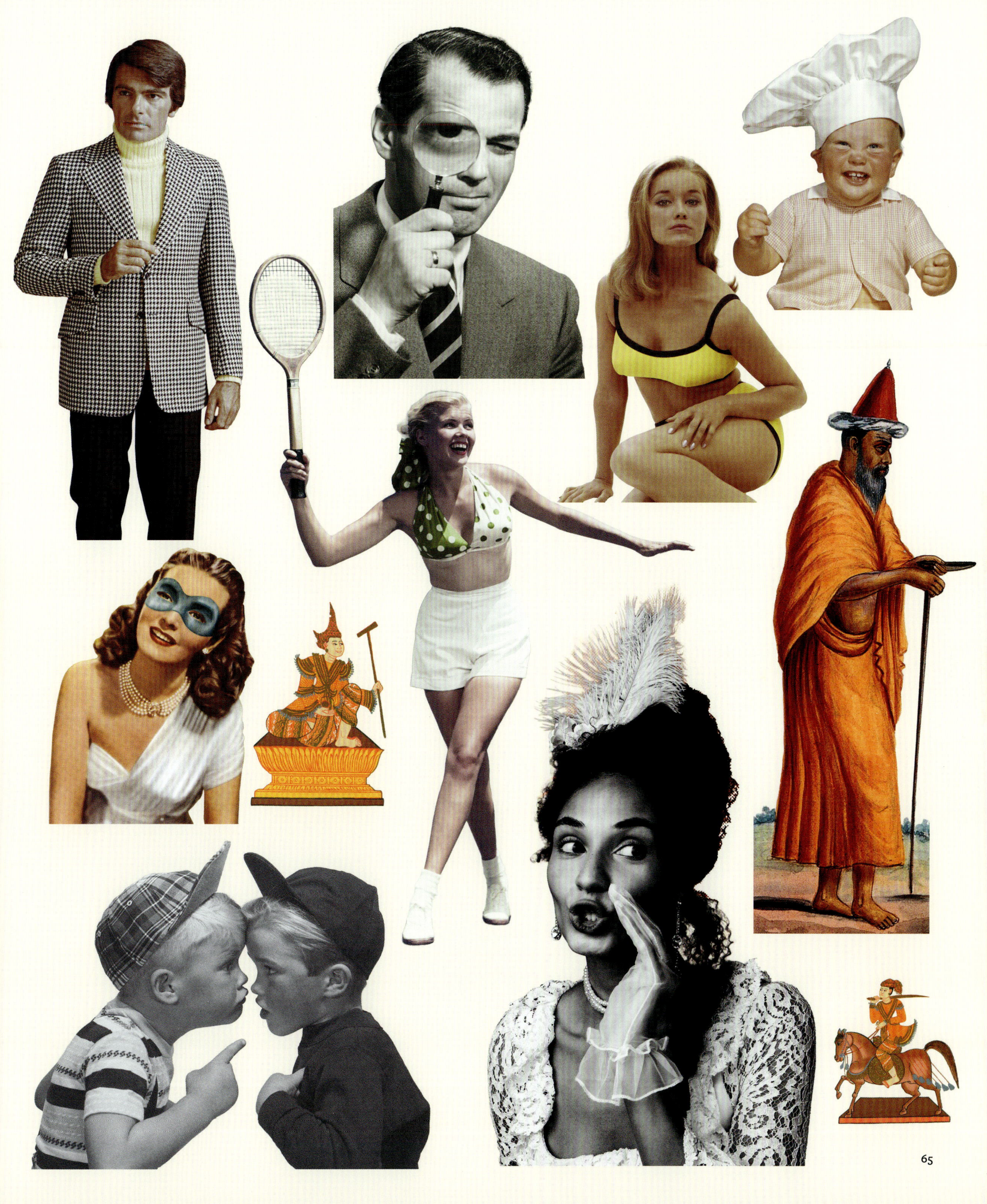

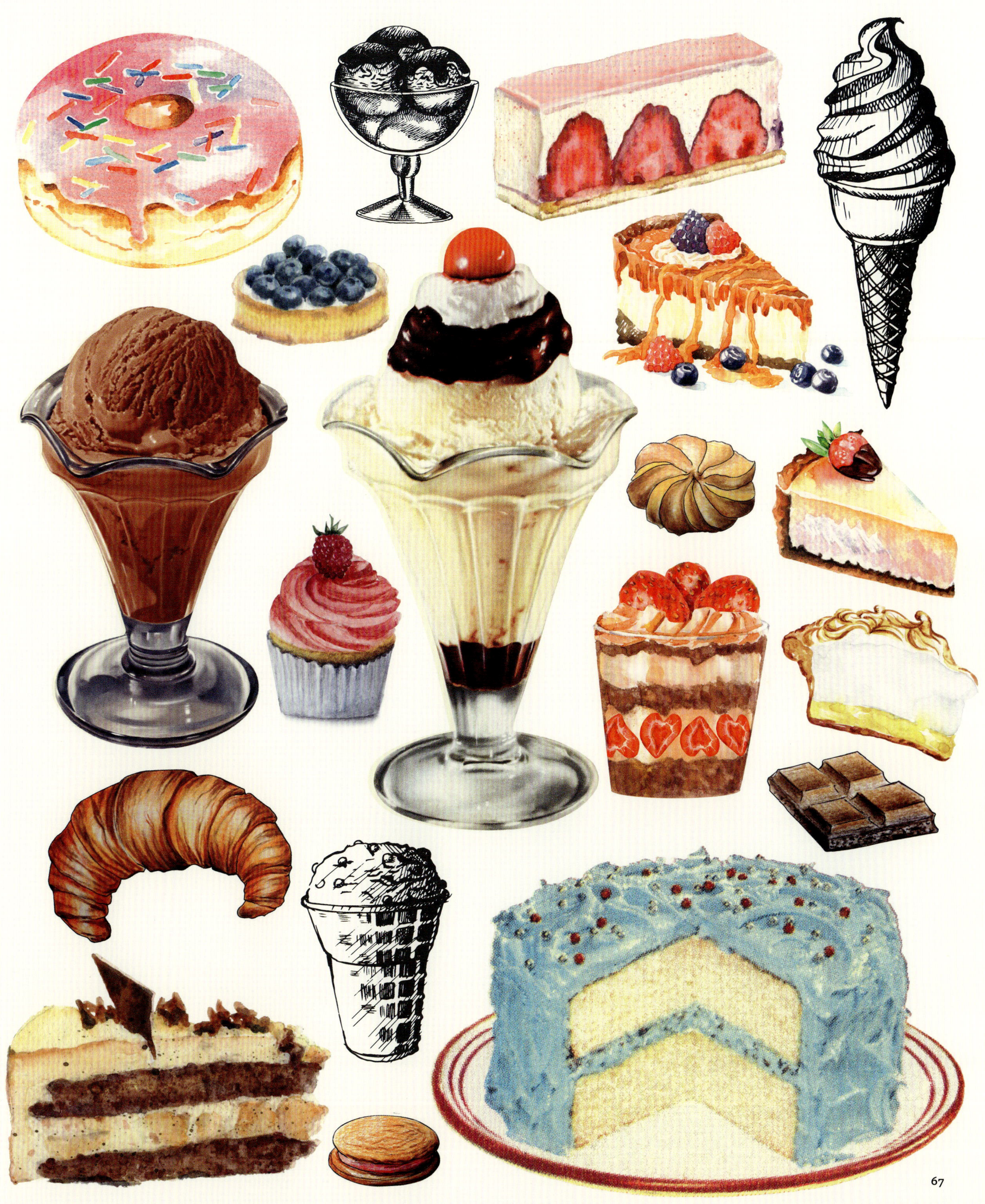

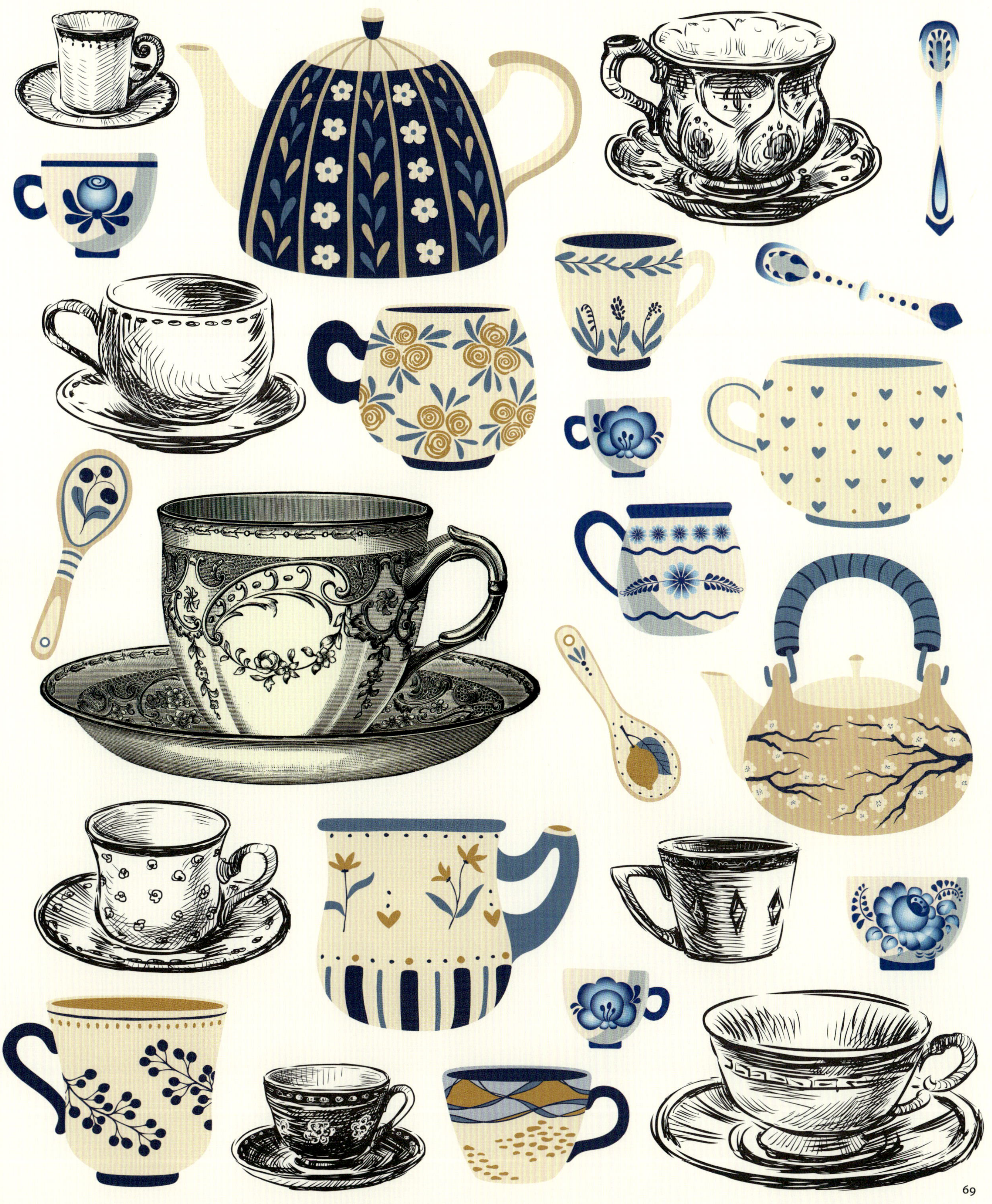

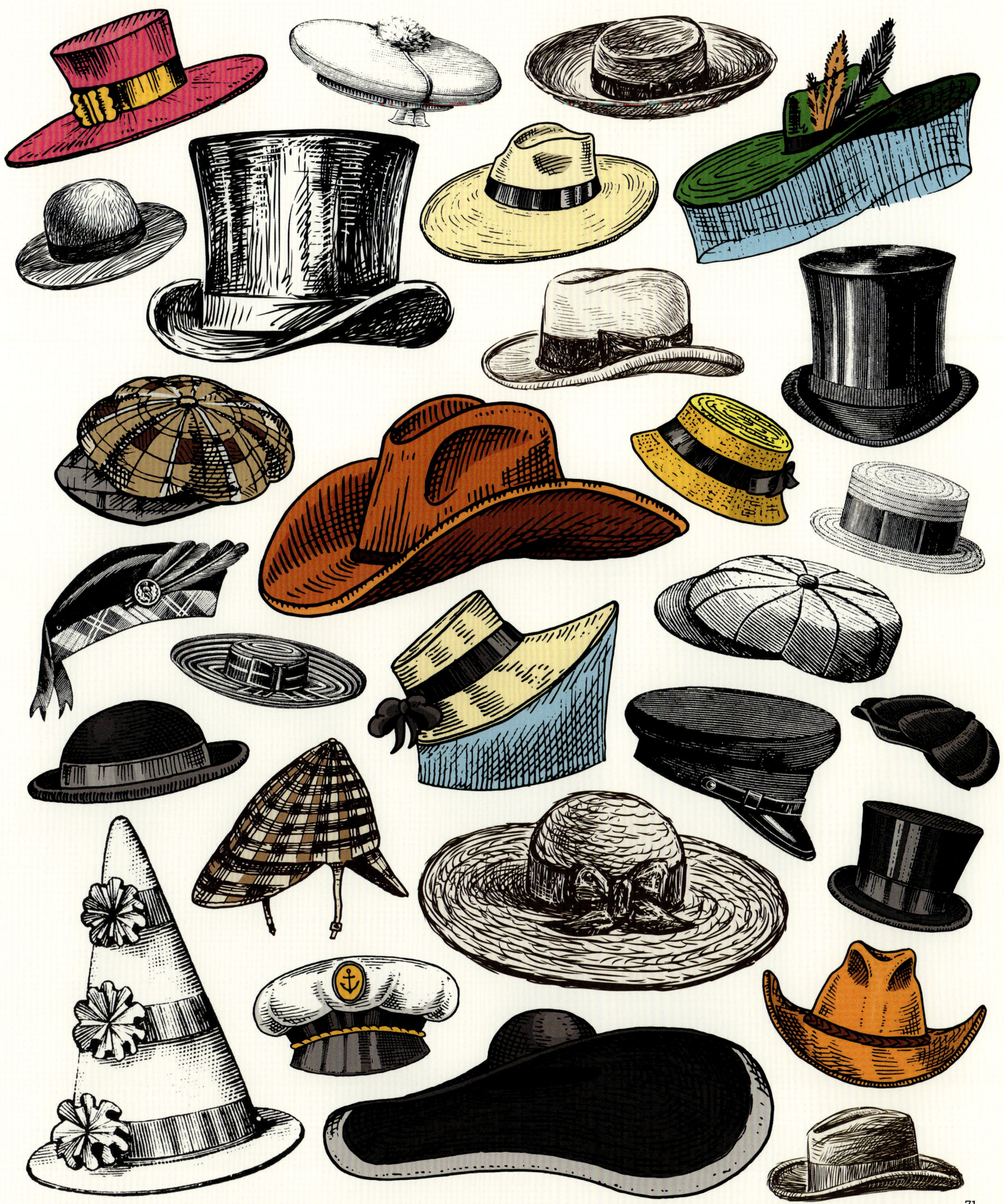

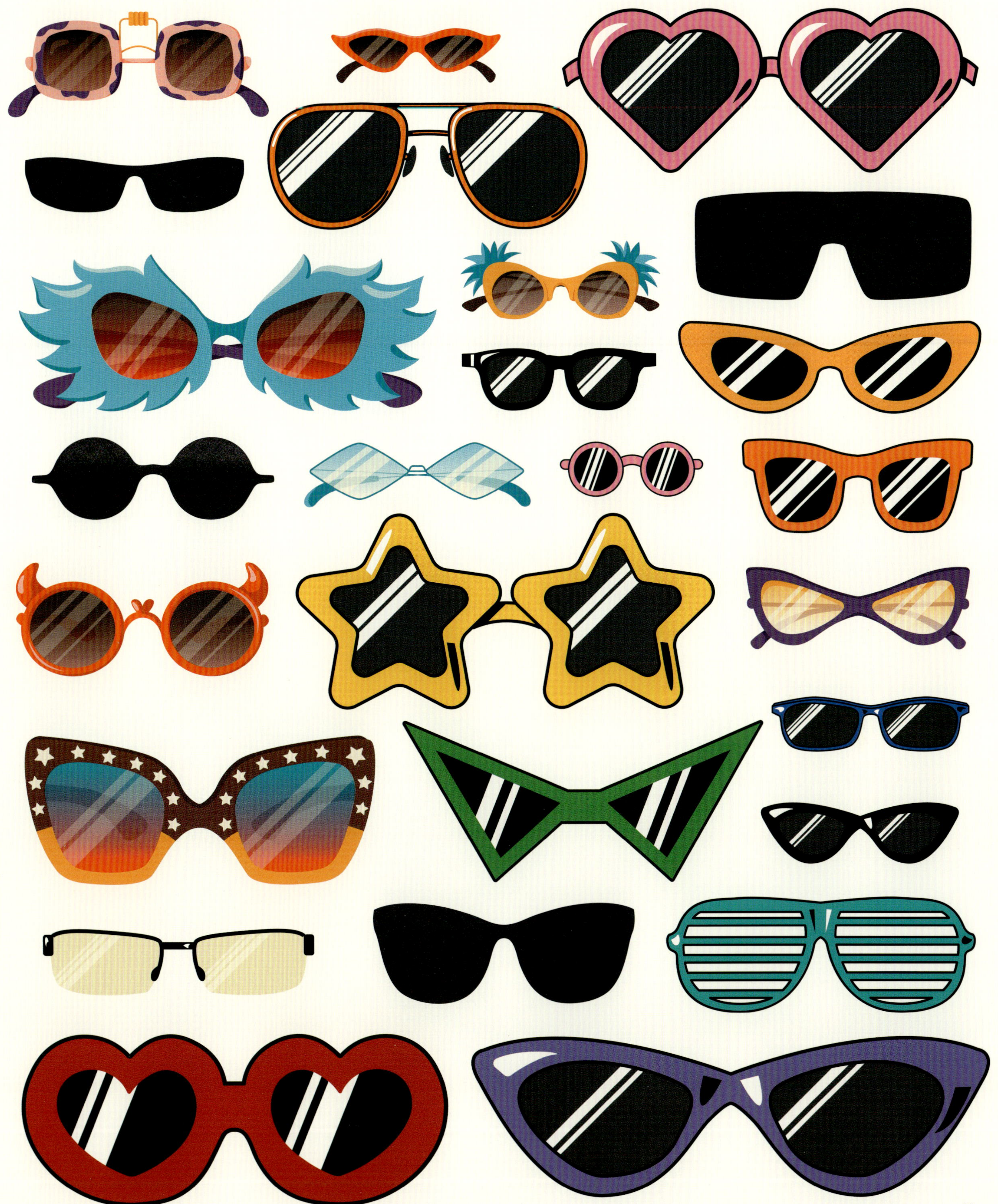

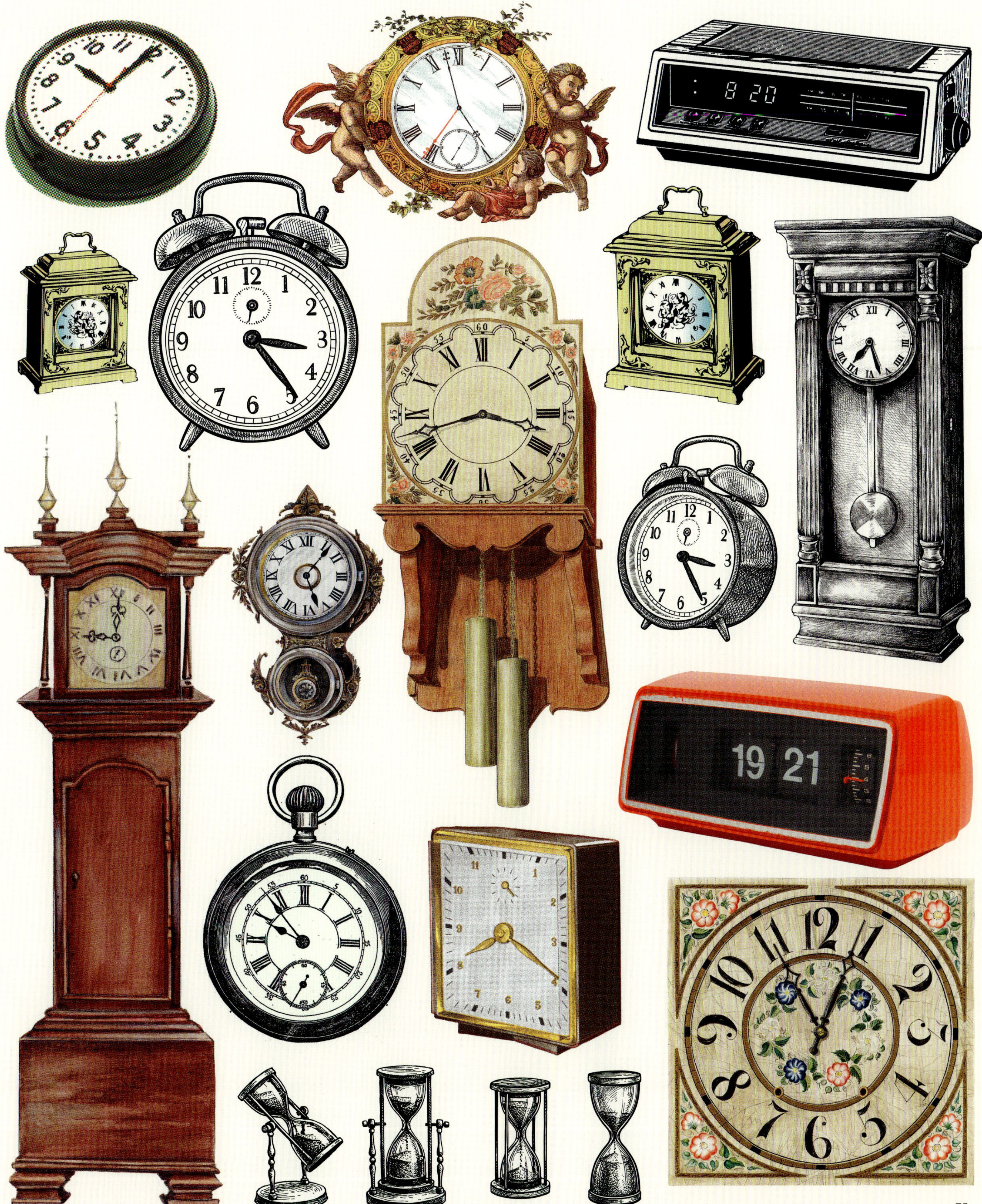
8 20
19 21

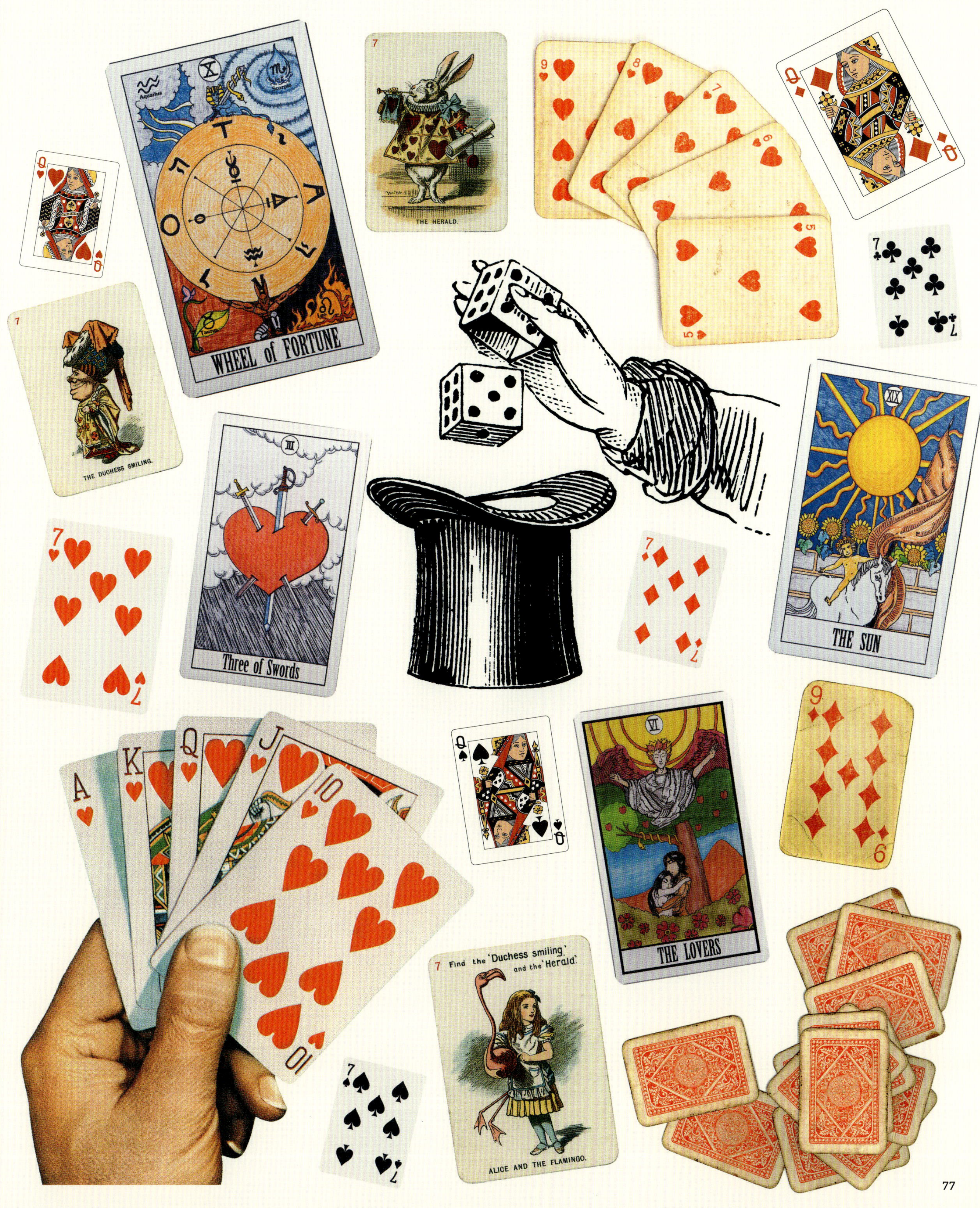

WHEEL of FORTUNE
THE HERALD.
THE DUCHESS SMILING.
Three of Swords
THE SUN
THE LOVERS
Find the 'Duchess smiling' and the 'Herald'.
ALICE AND THE FLAMINGO.

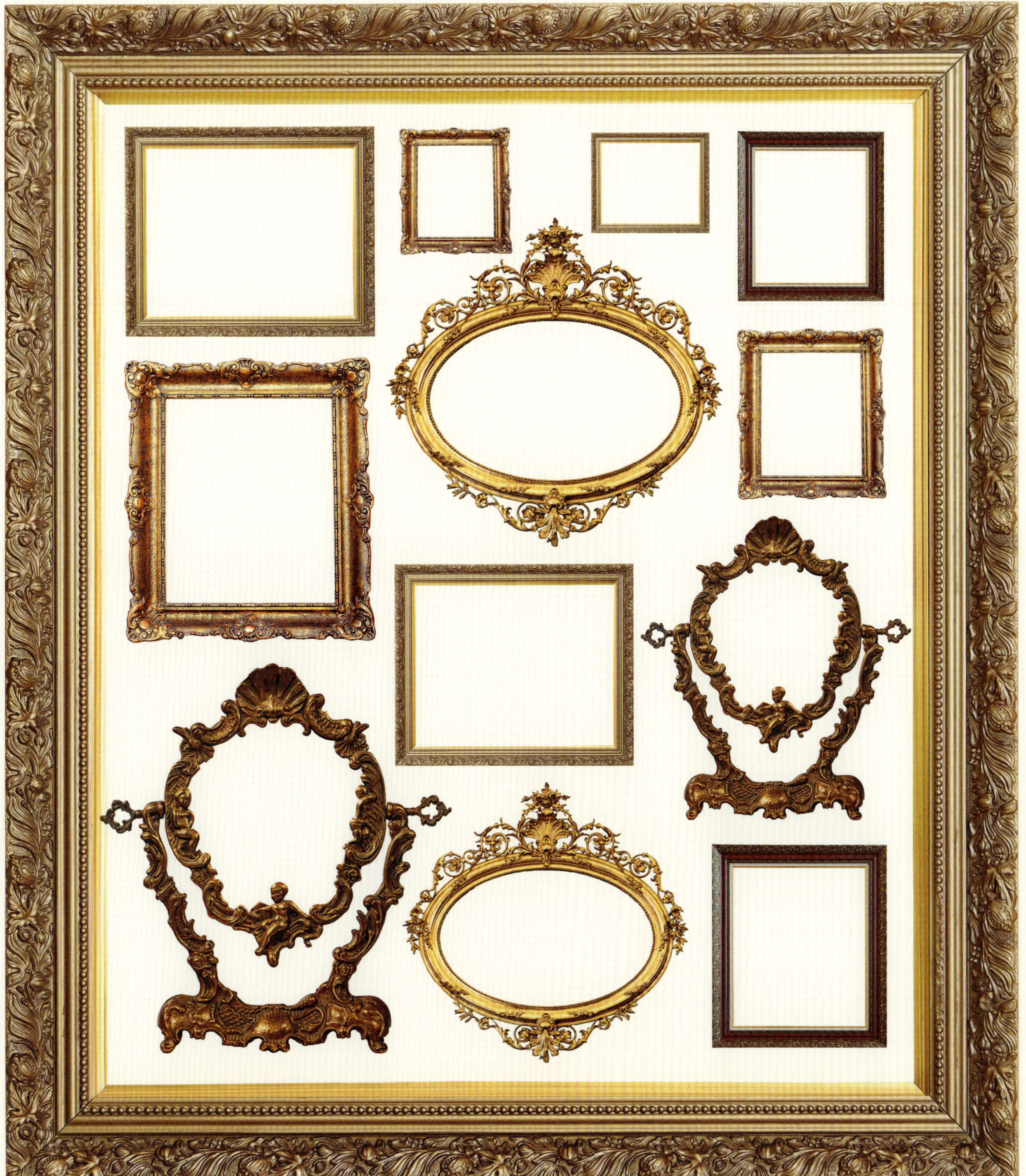

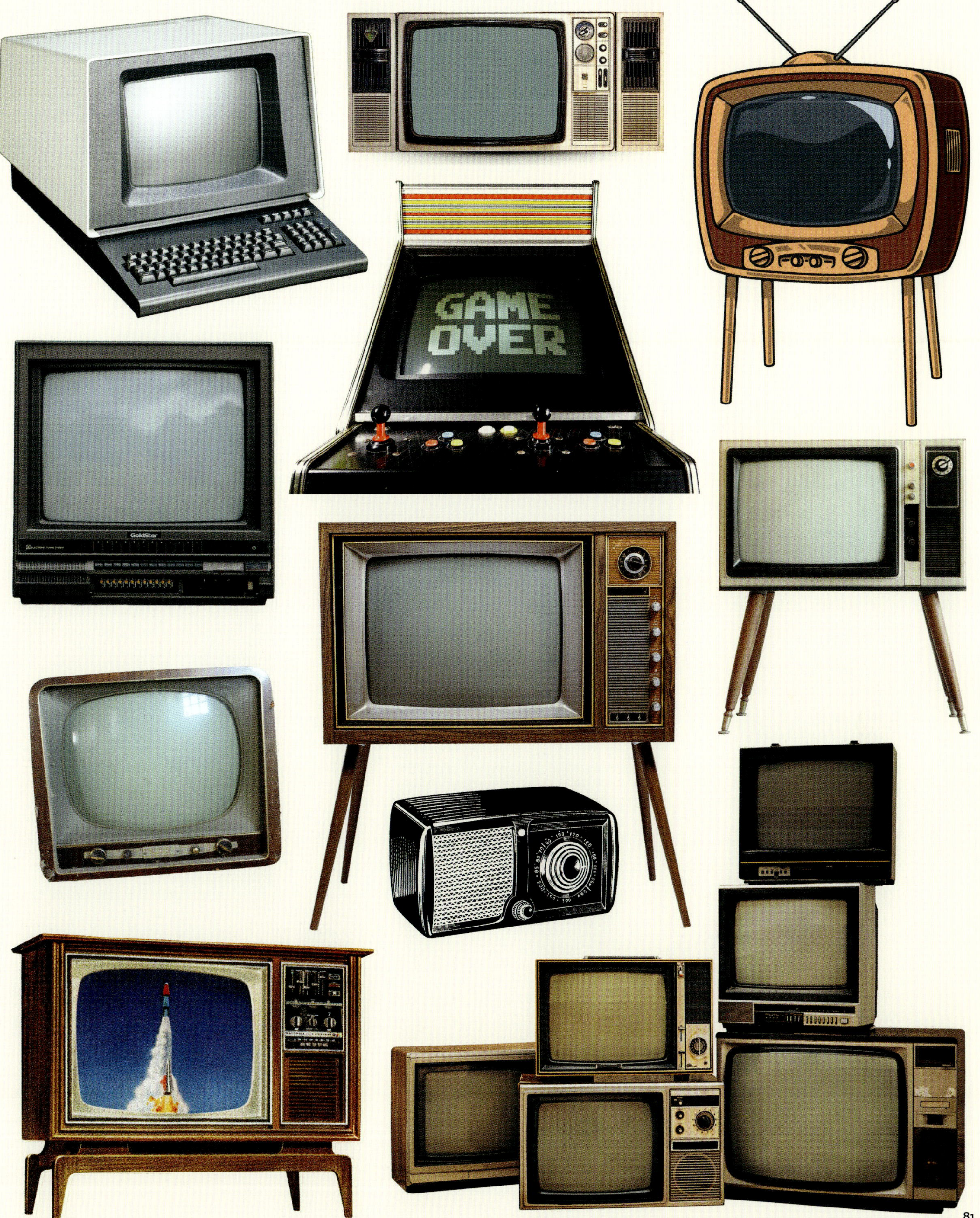
GAME
OVER
GoldStar

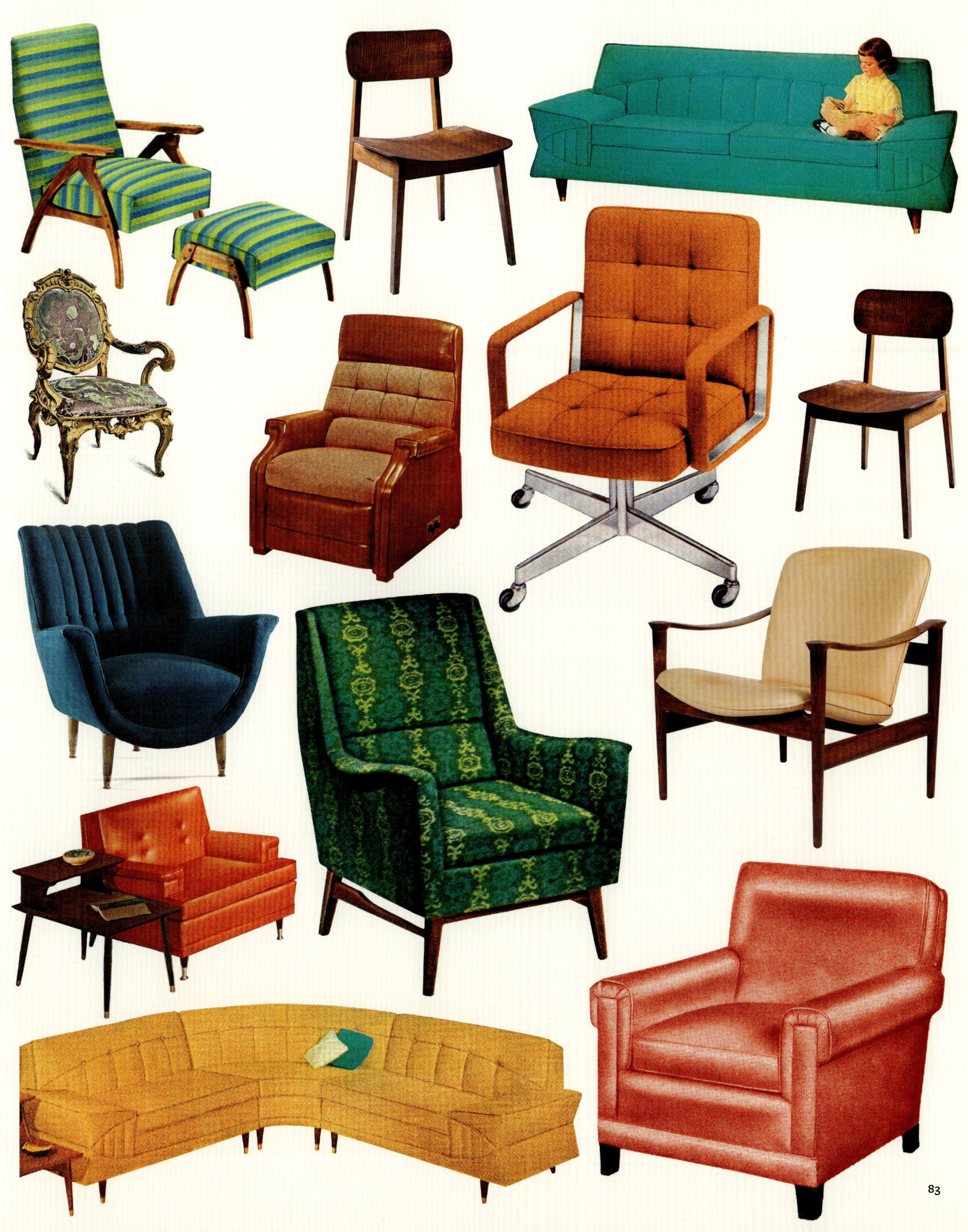

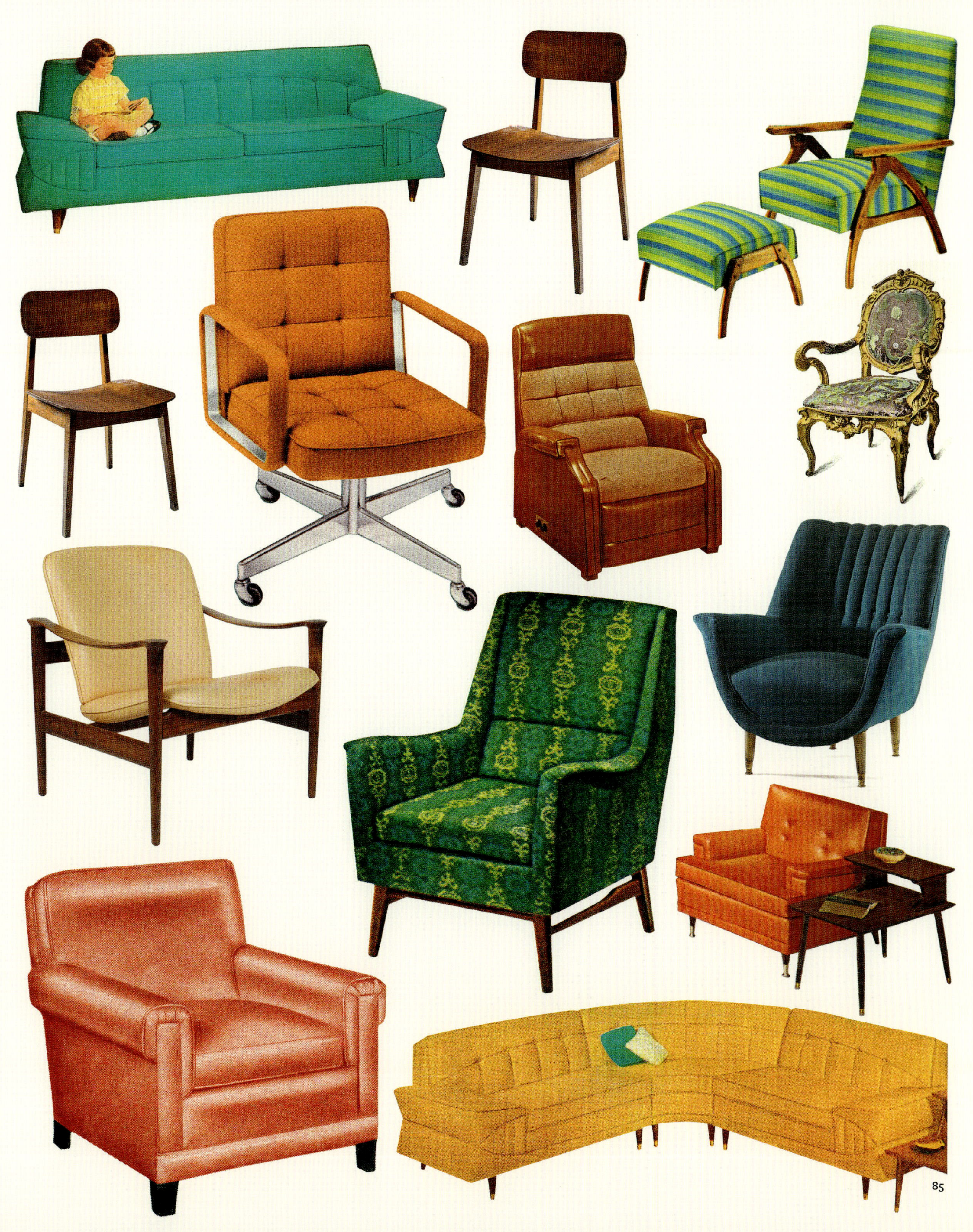

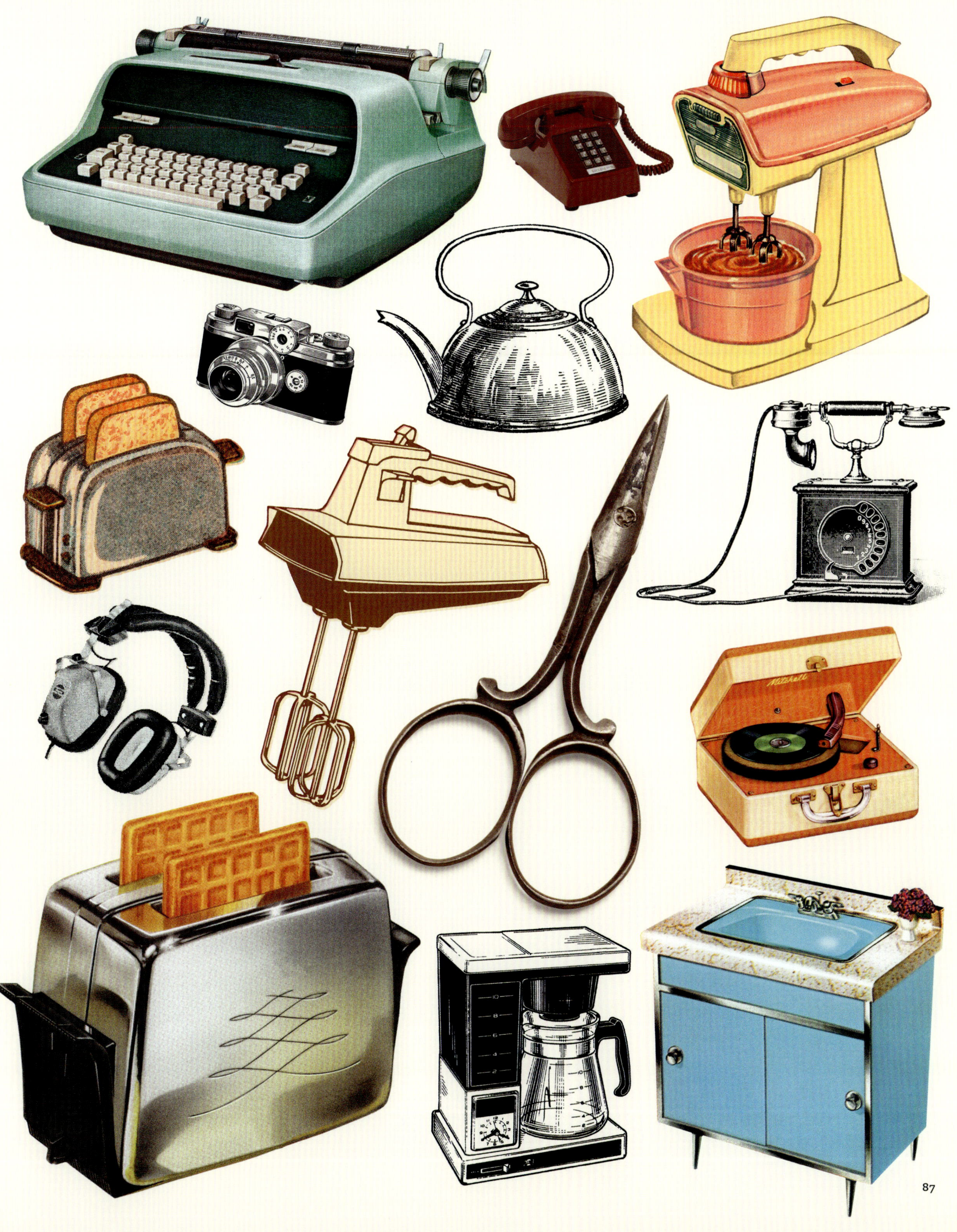
Mitchell

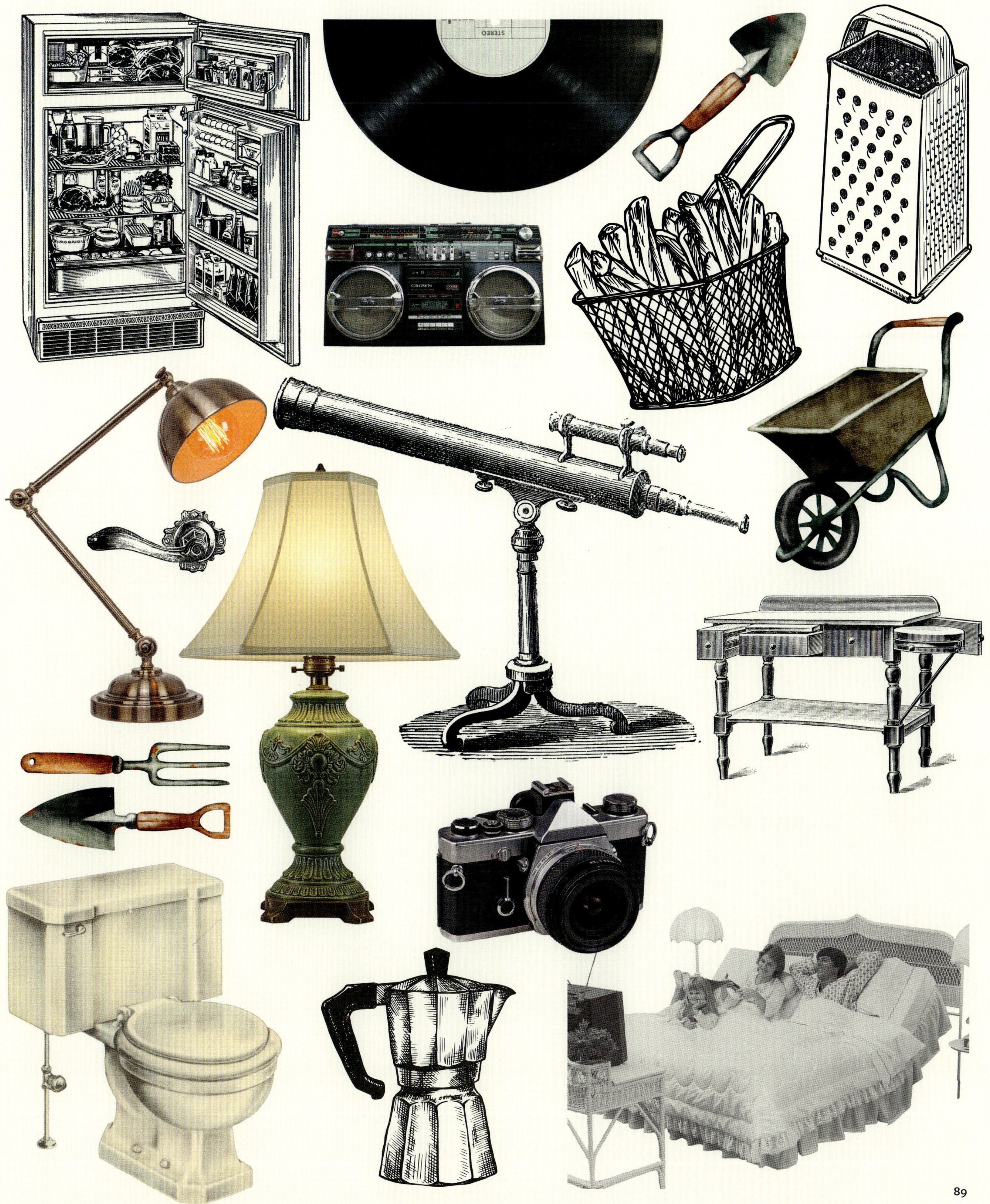

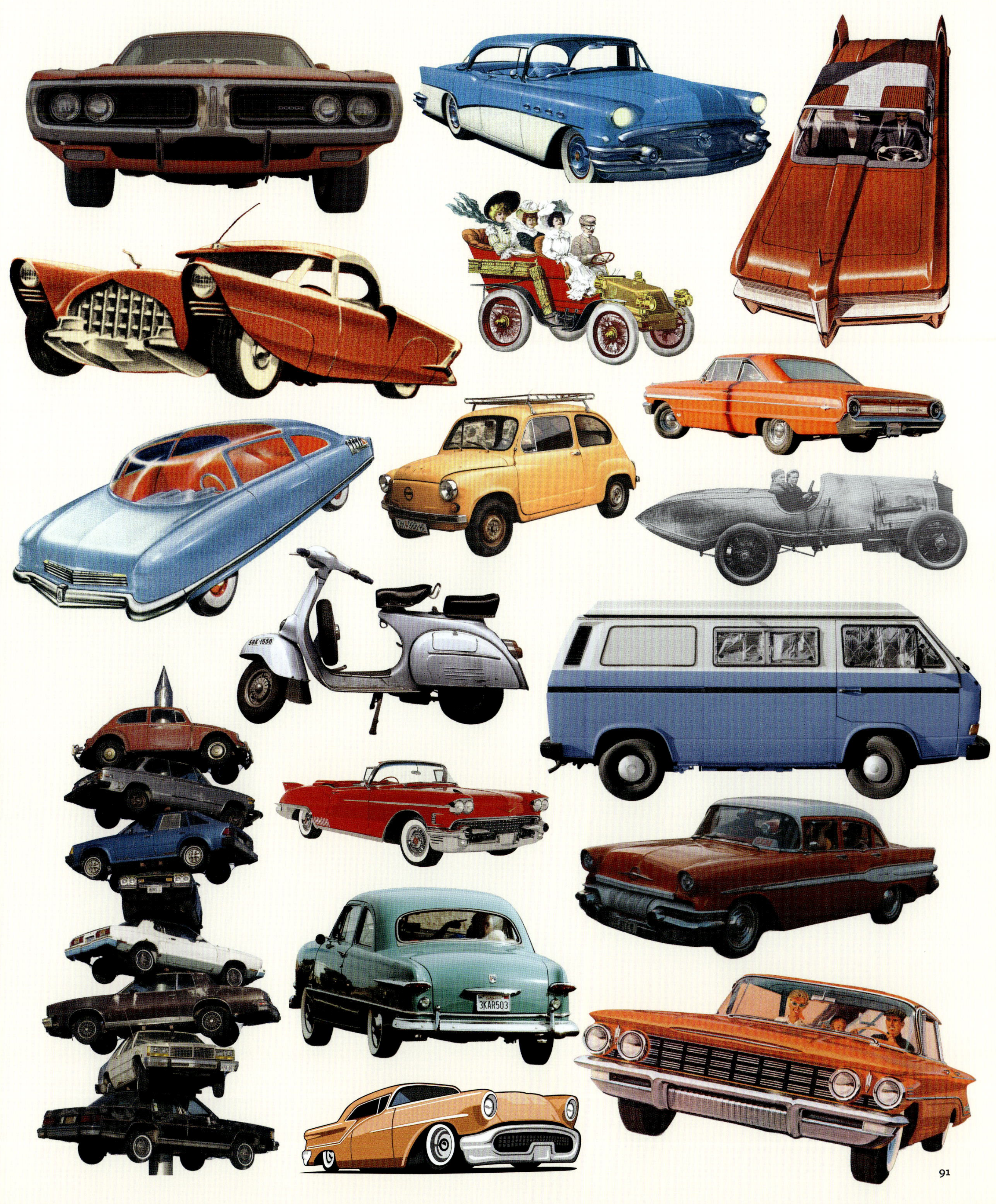

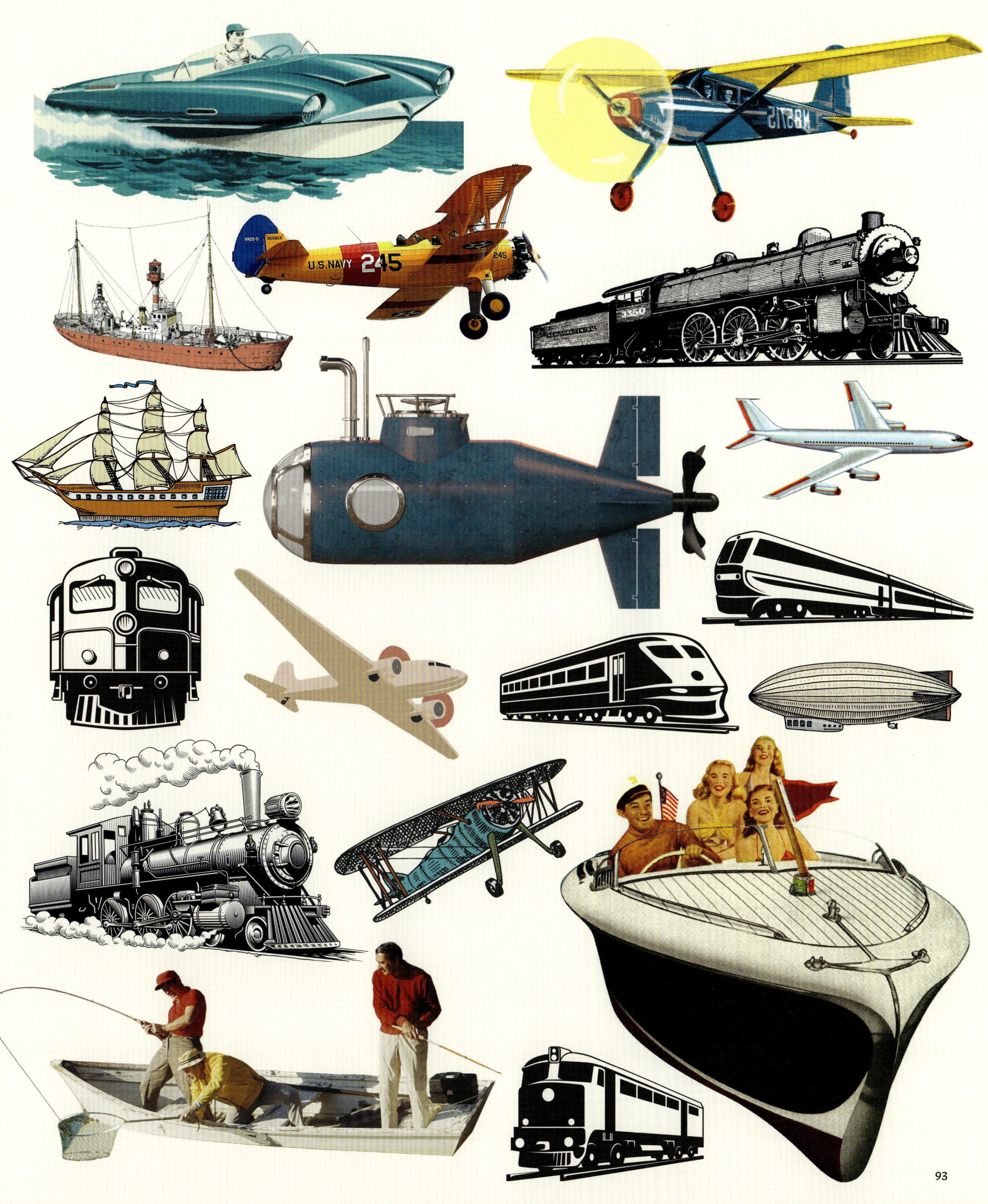
U.S.NAVY 245
245
3350
NEW YORK CENTRAL

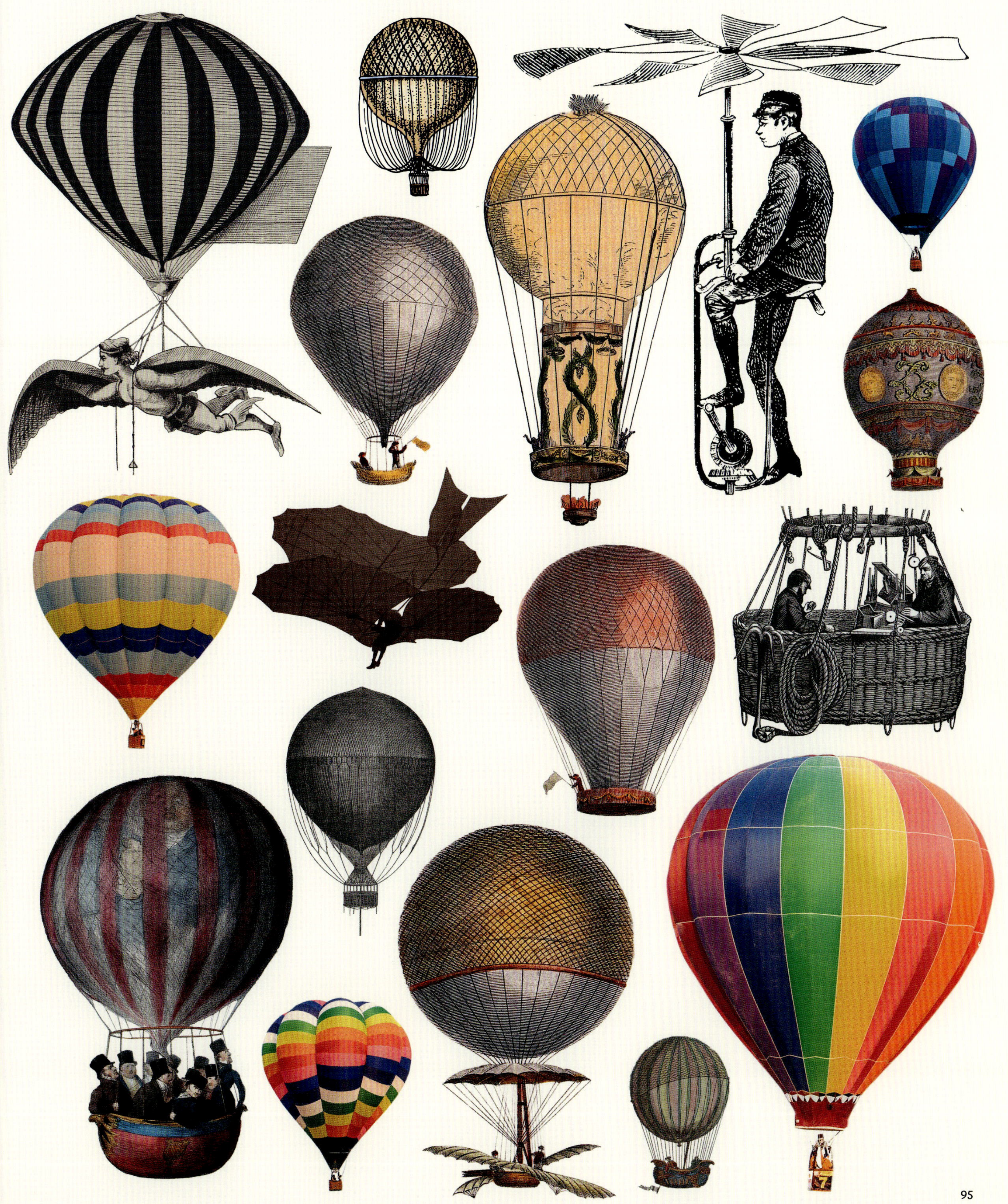

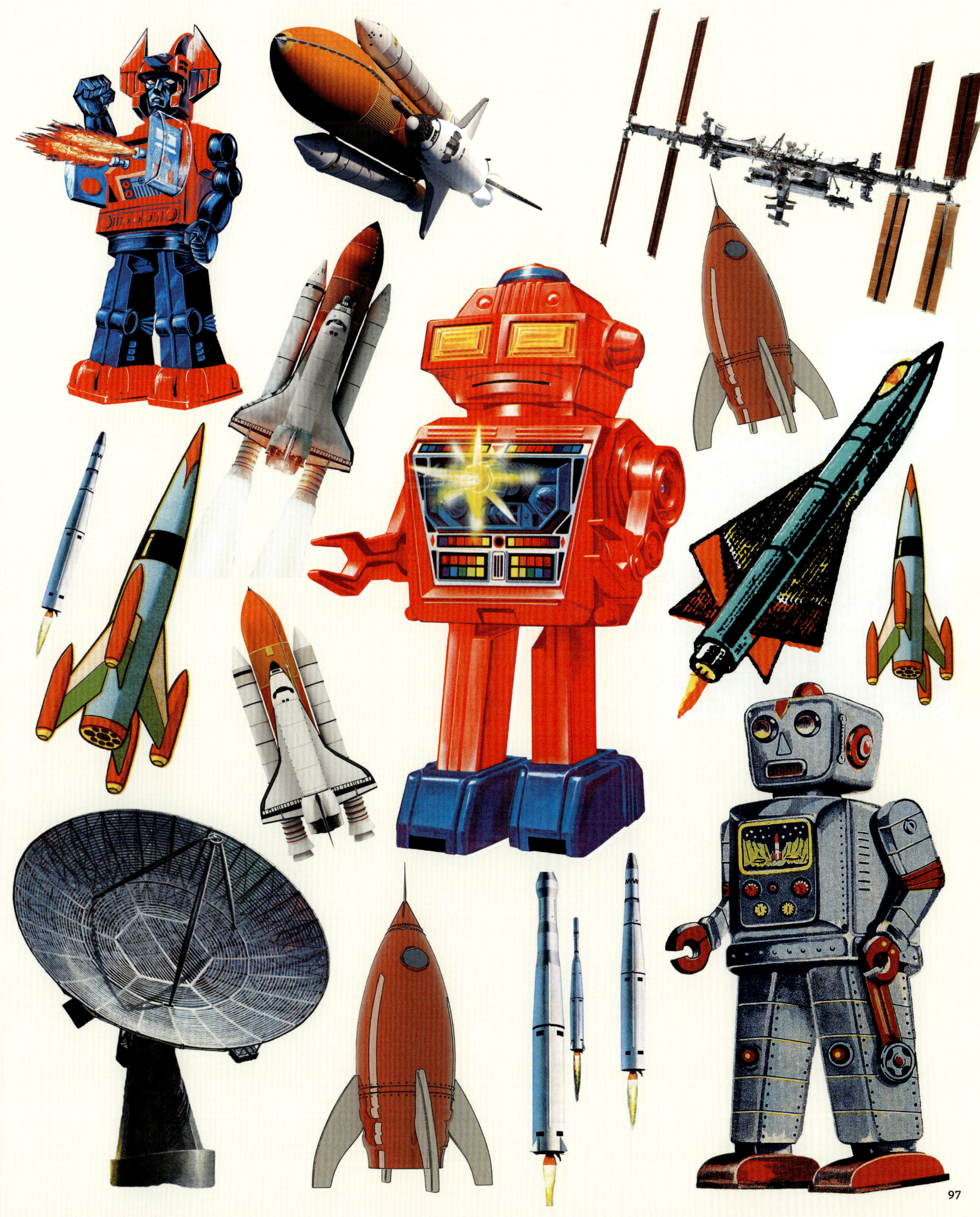

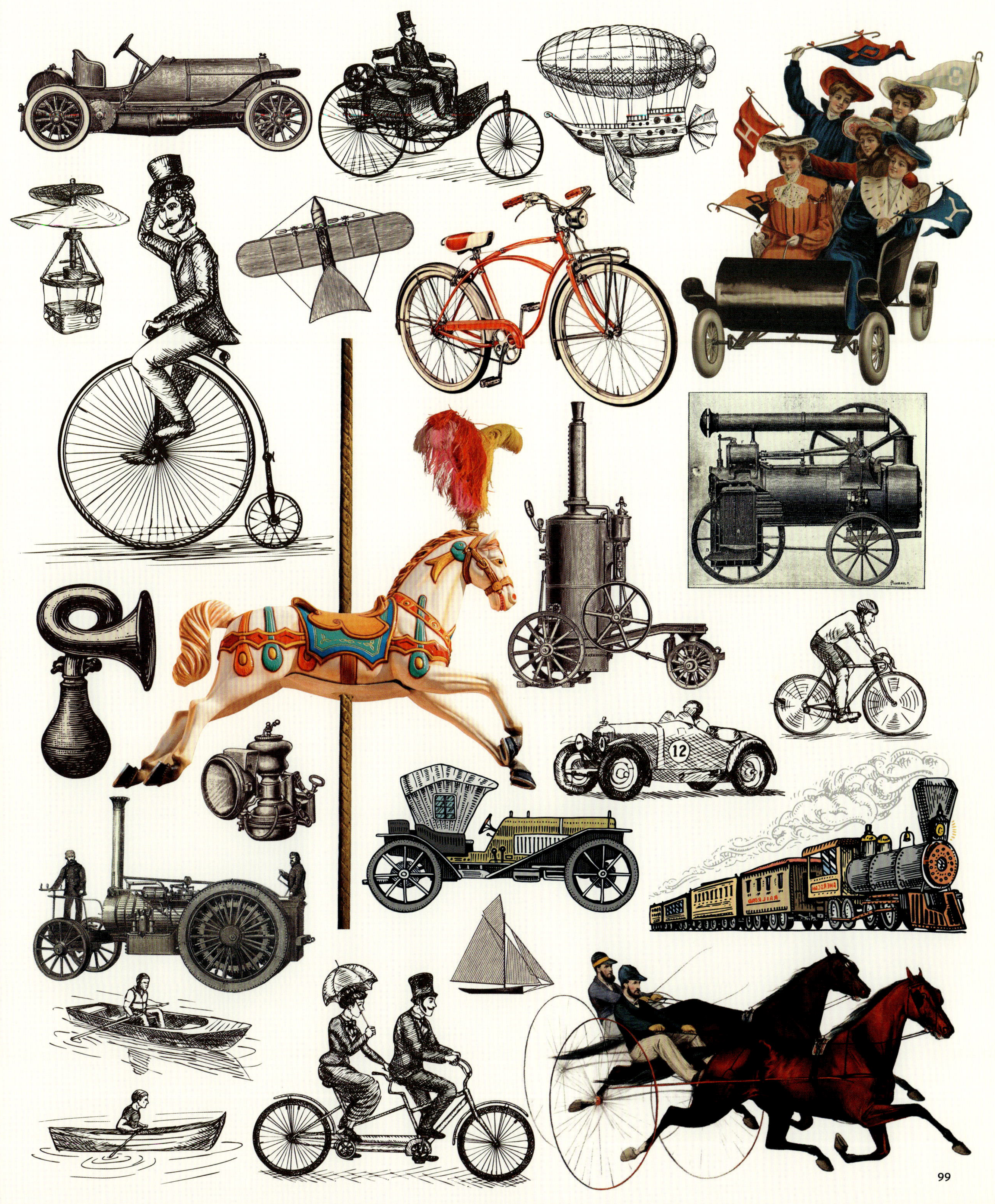
12

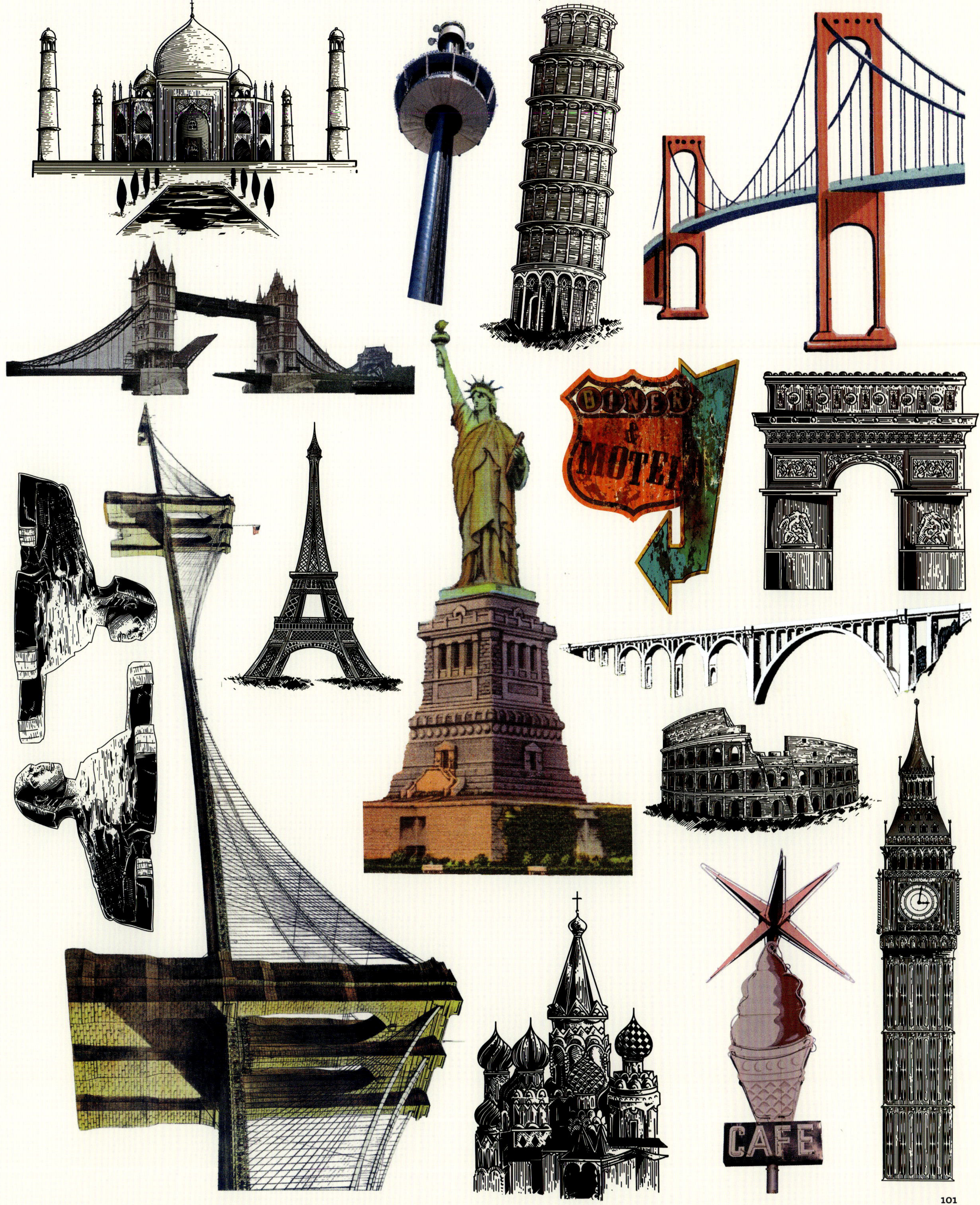
DINER
&
MOTEL
CAFE

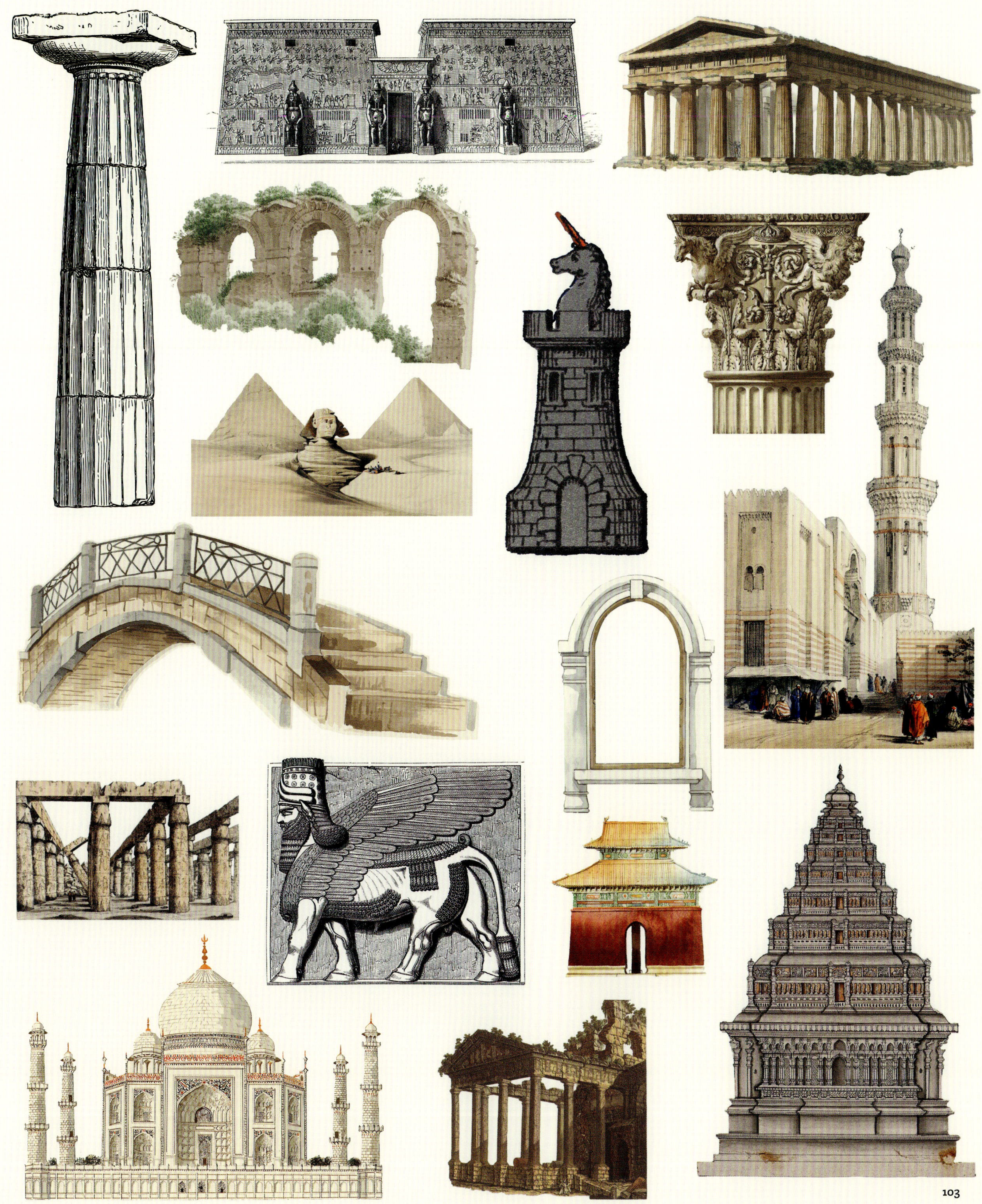

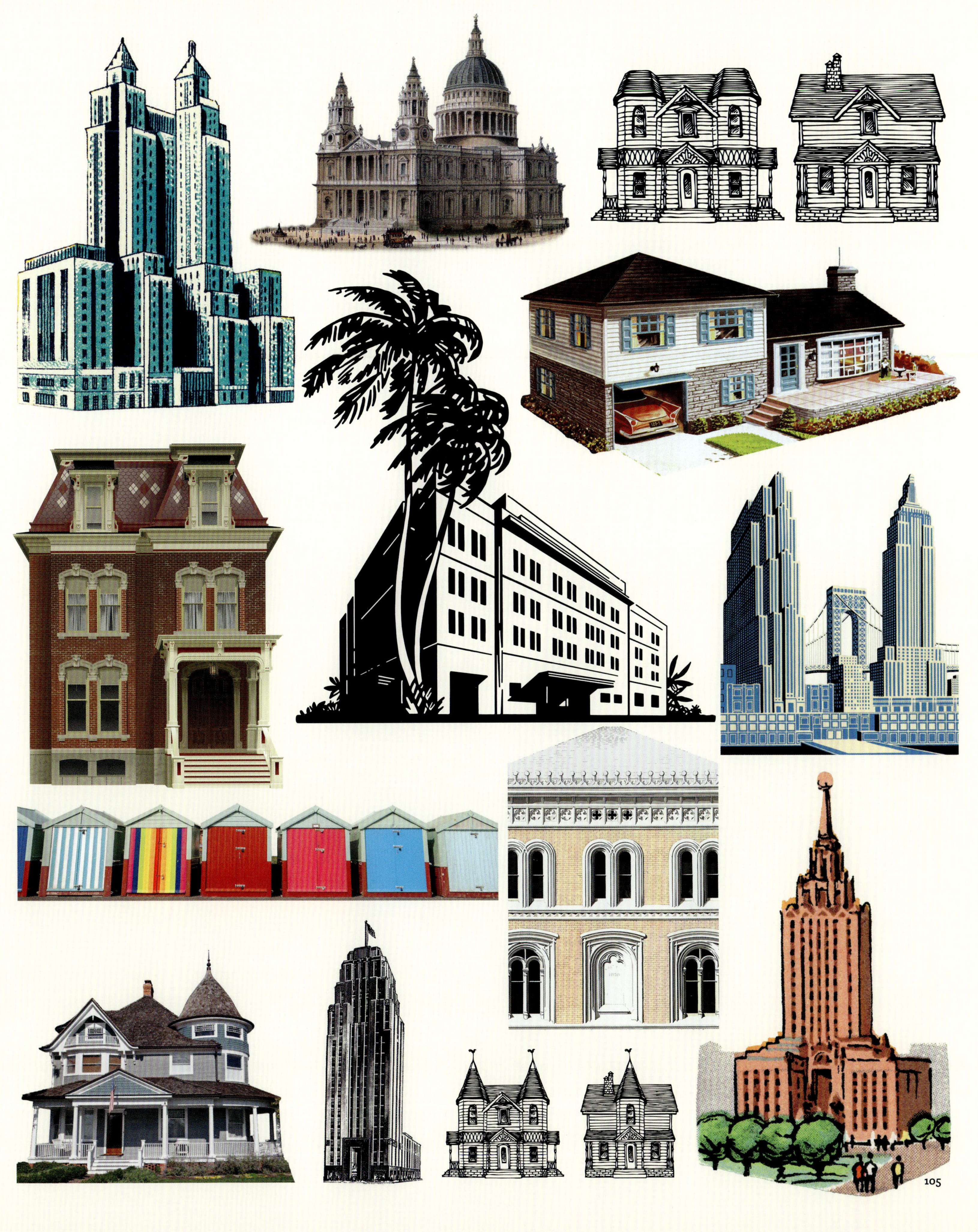

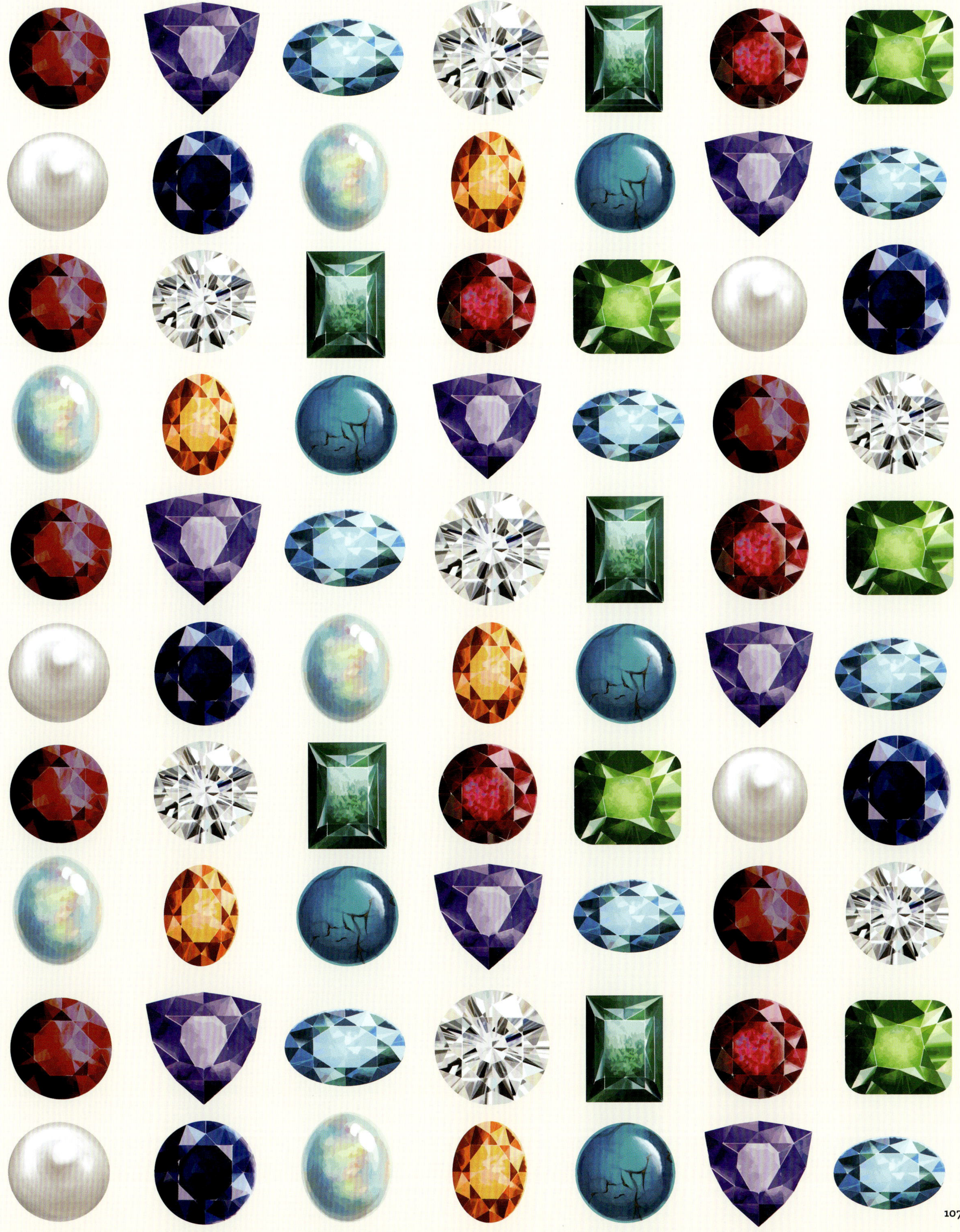

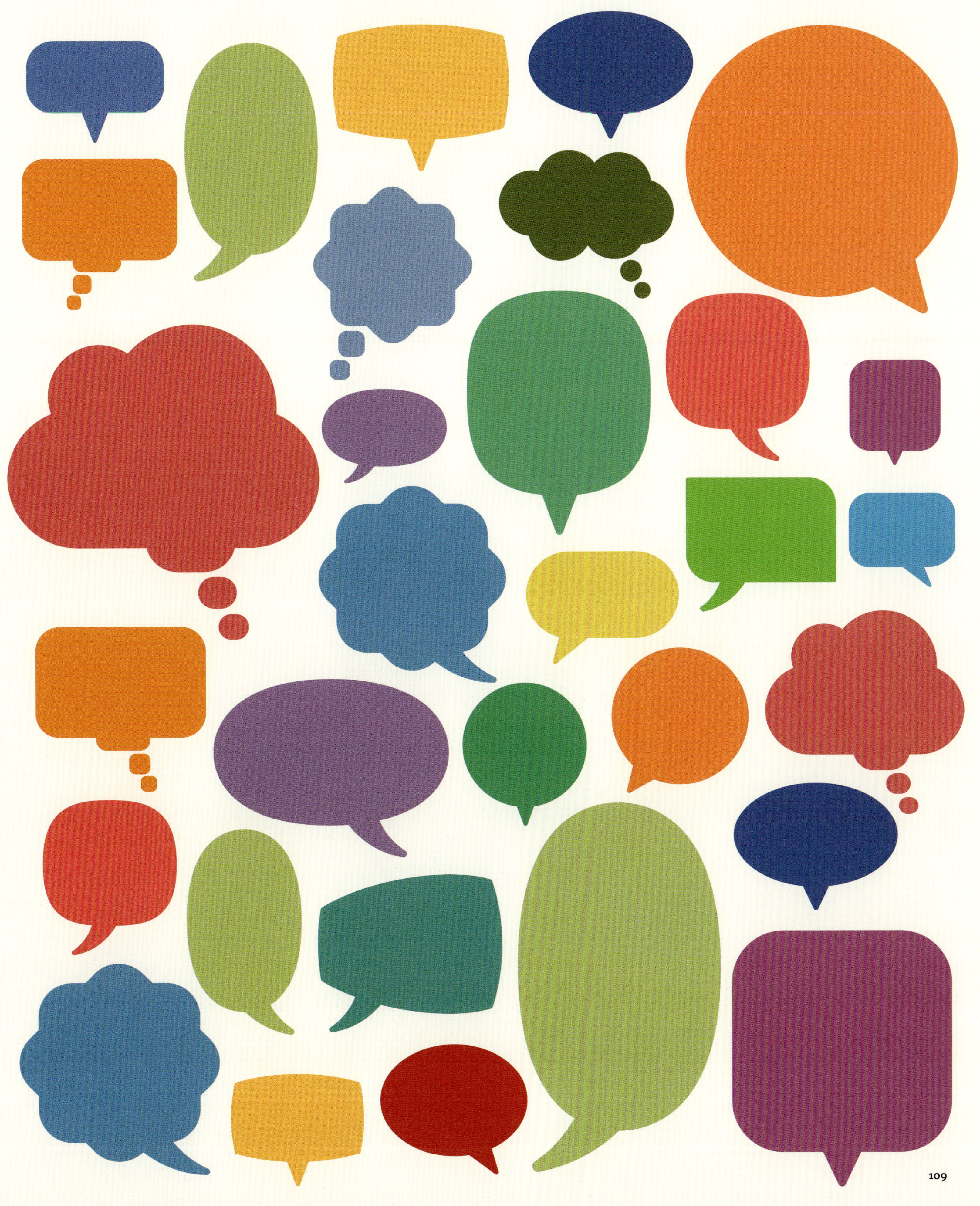

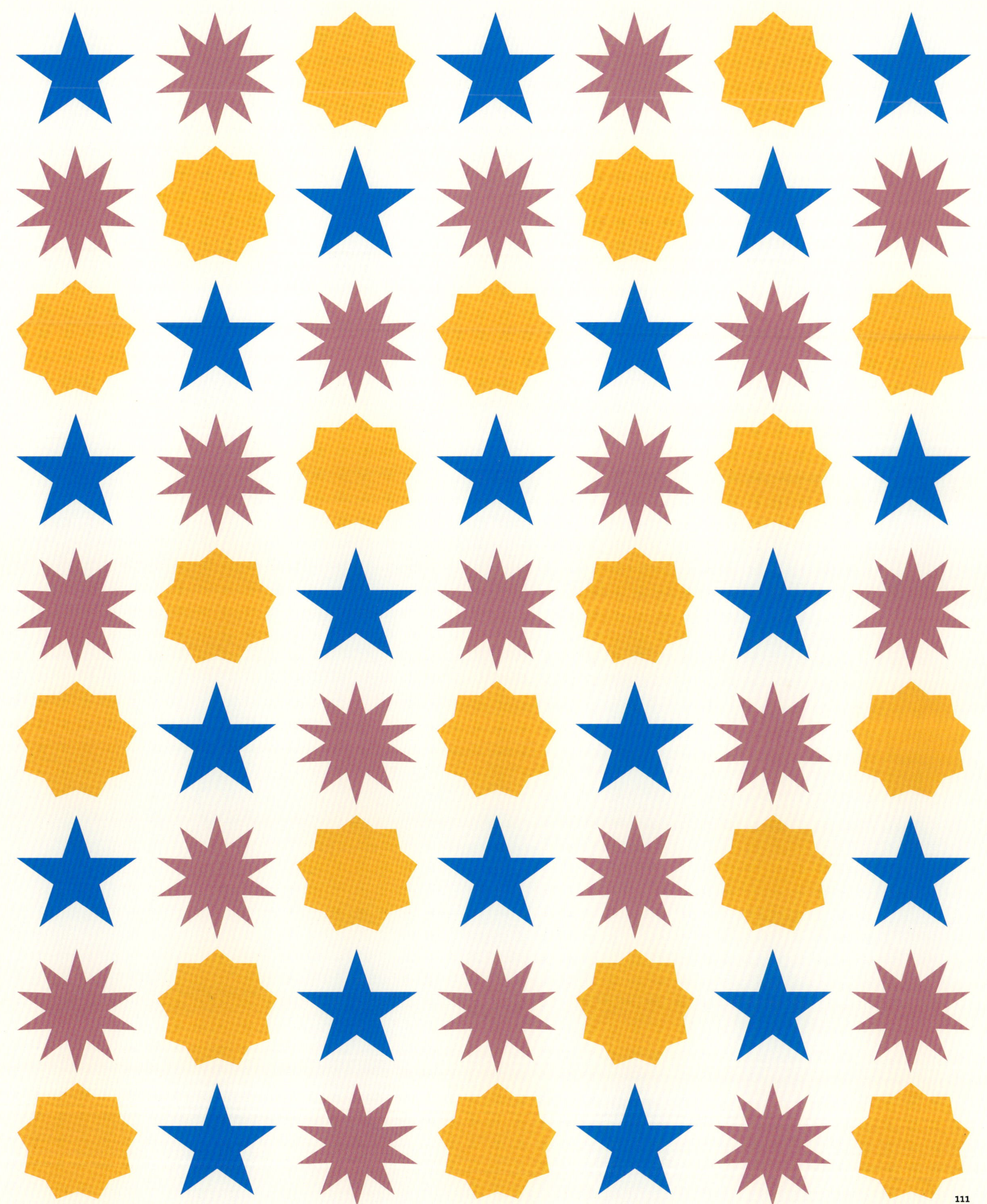

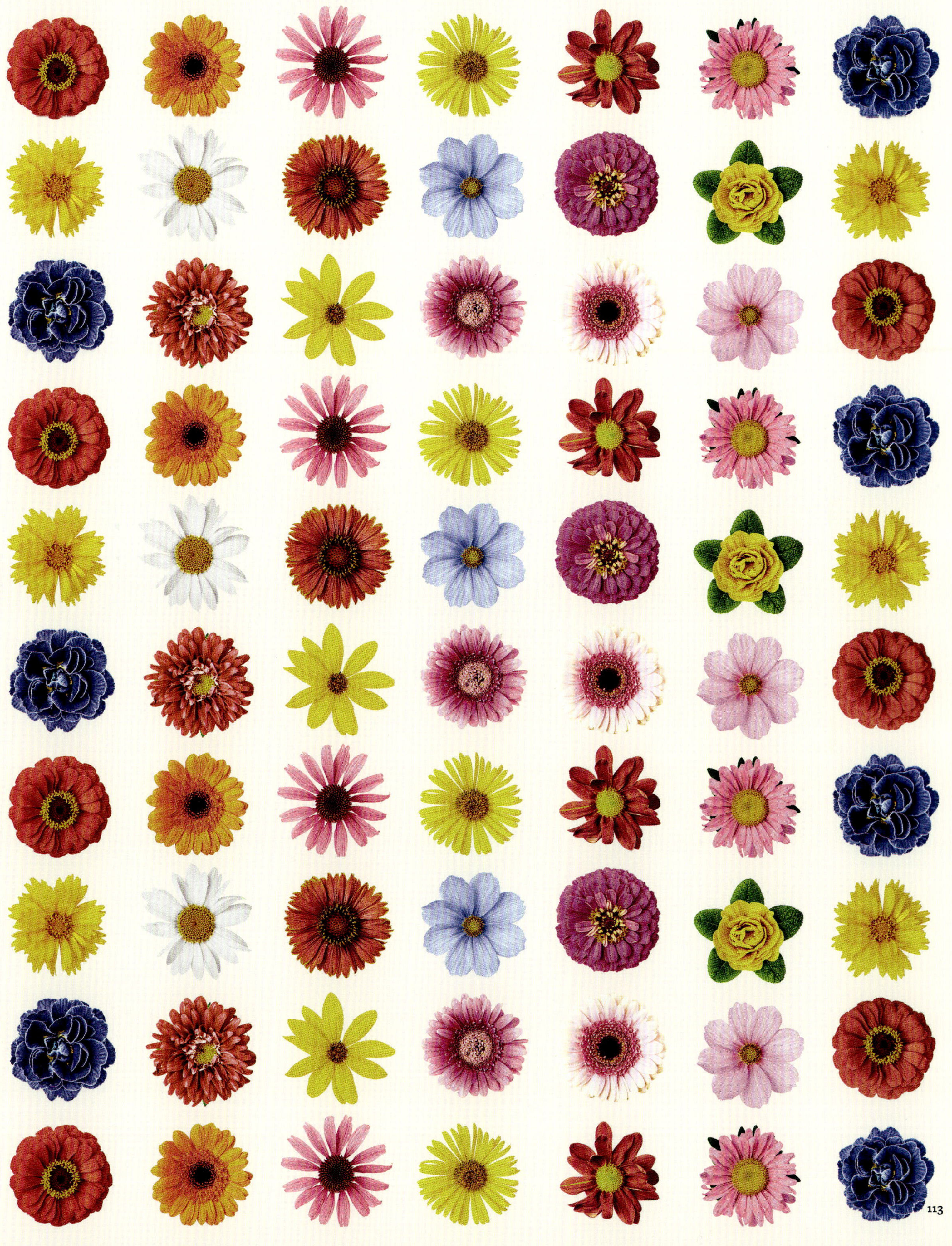

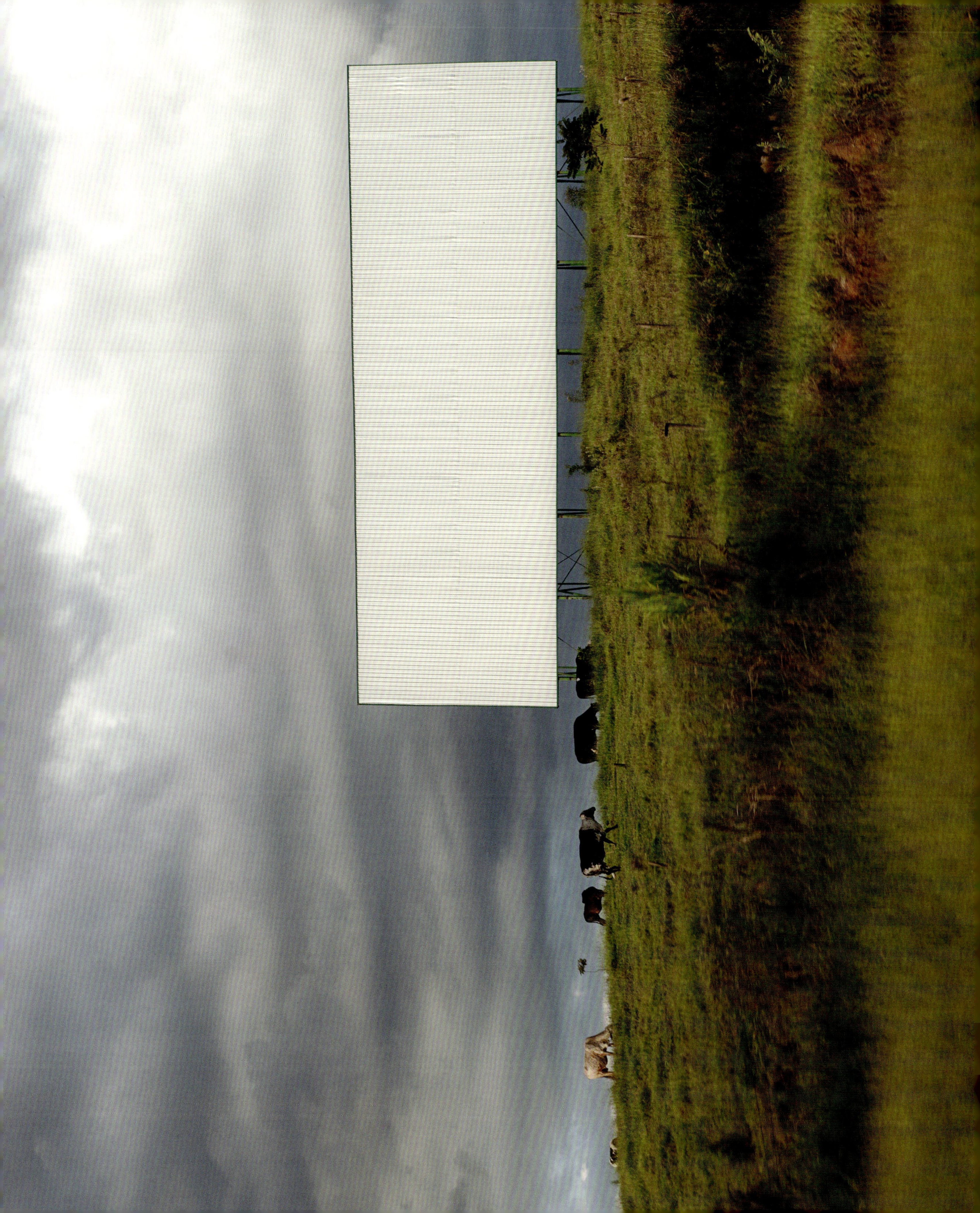

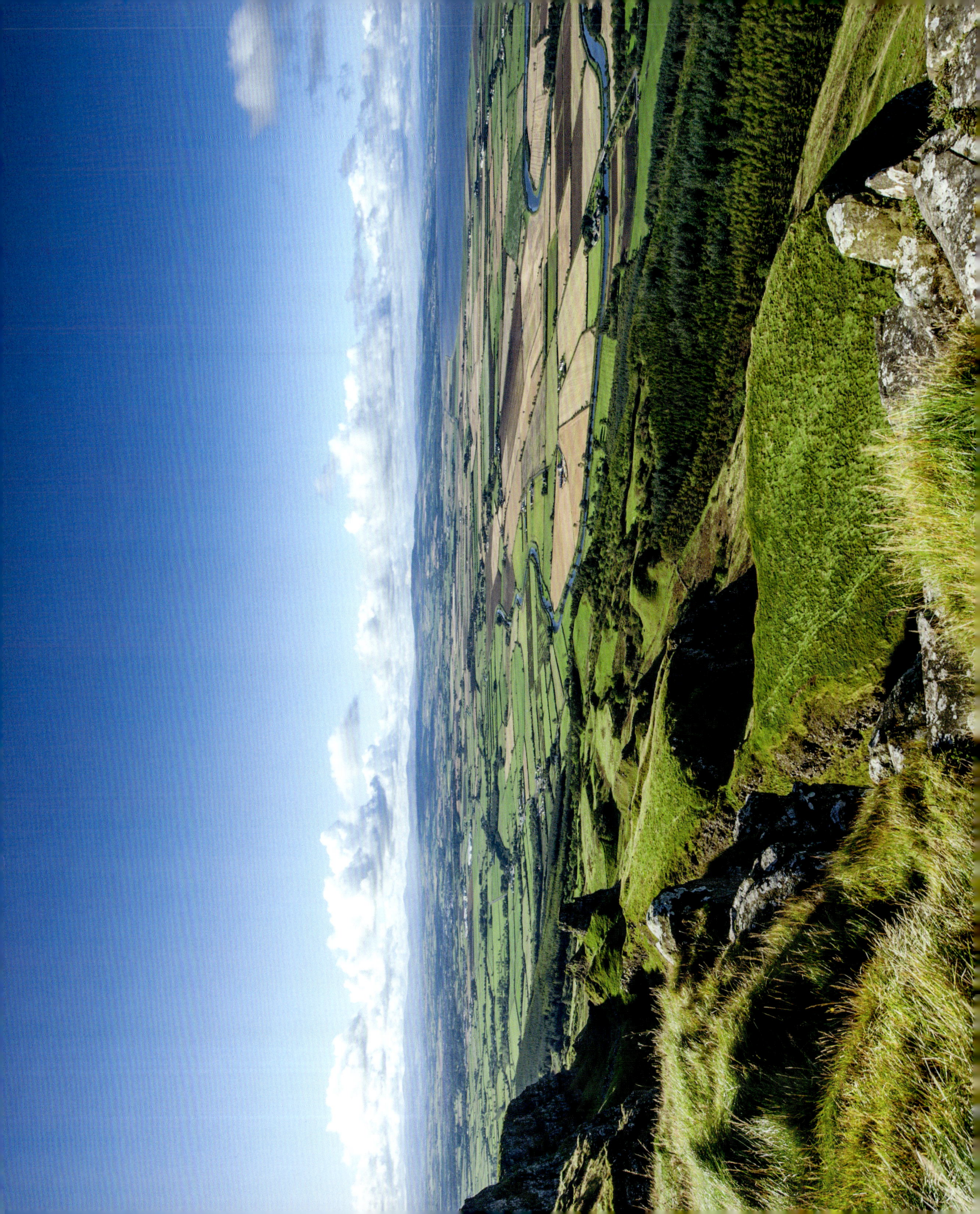

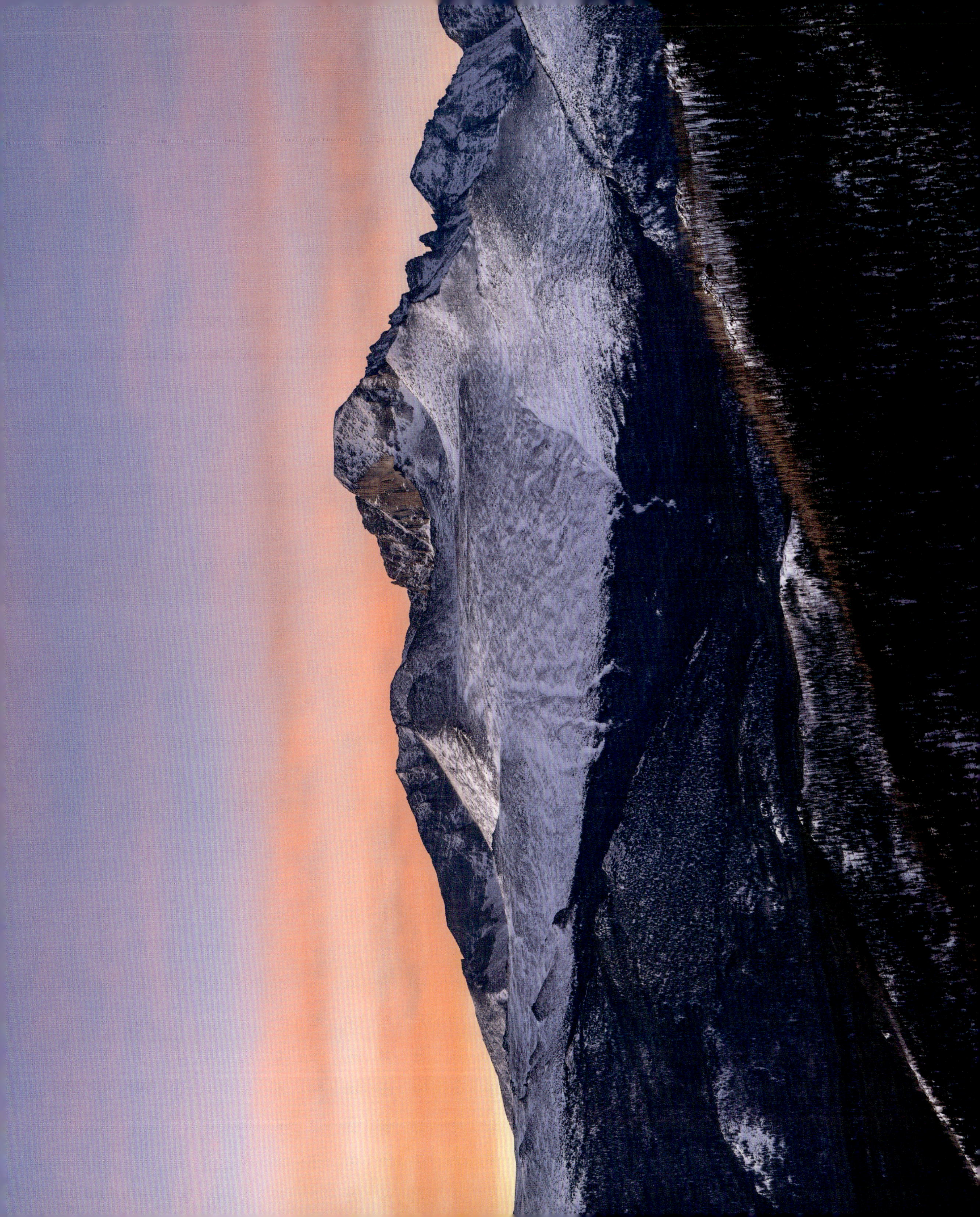

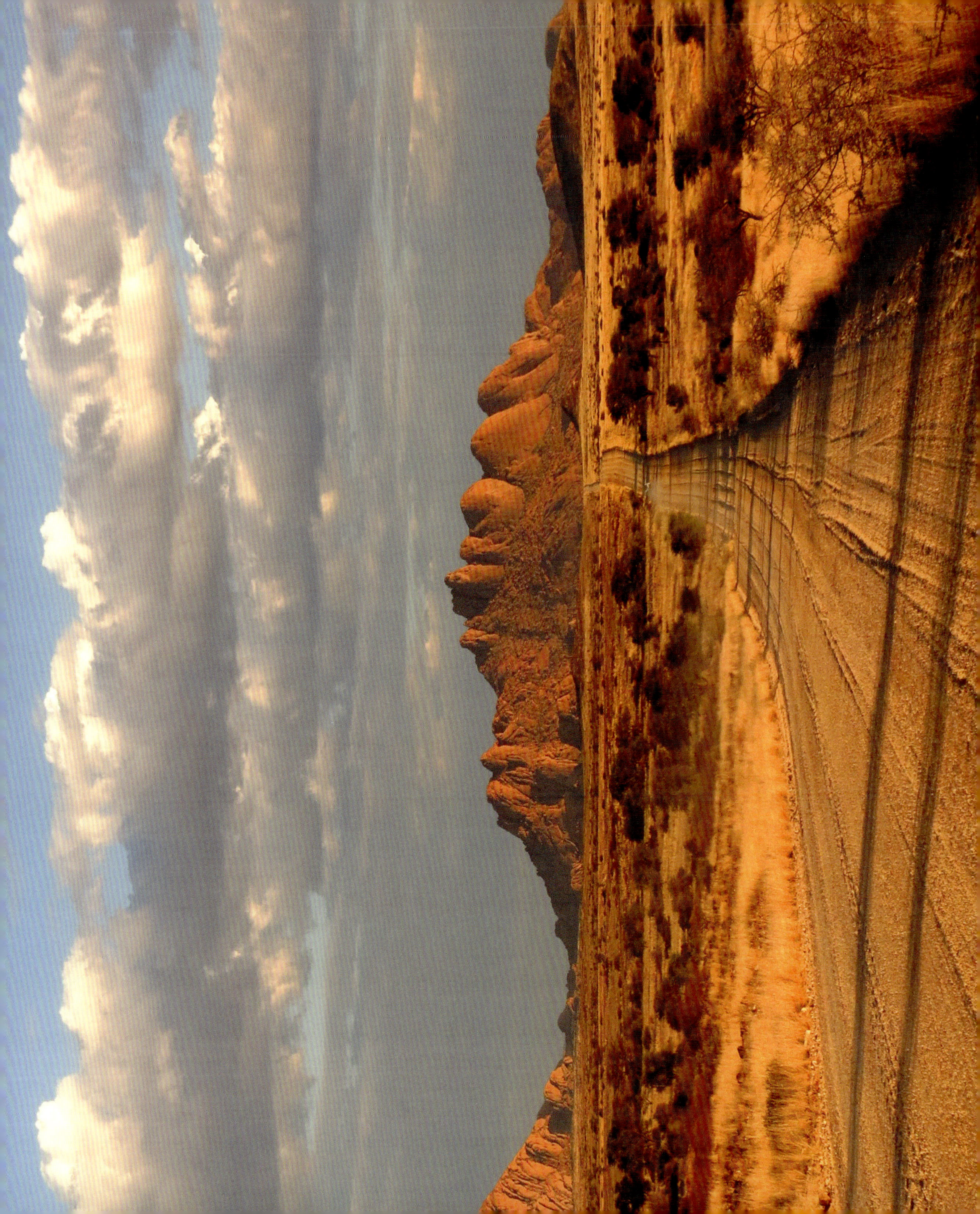

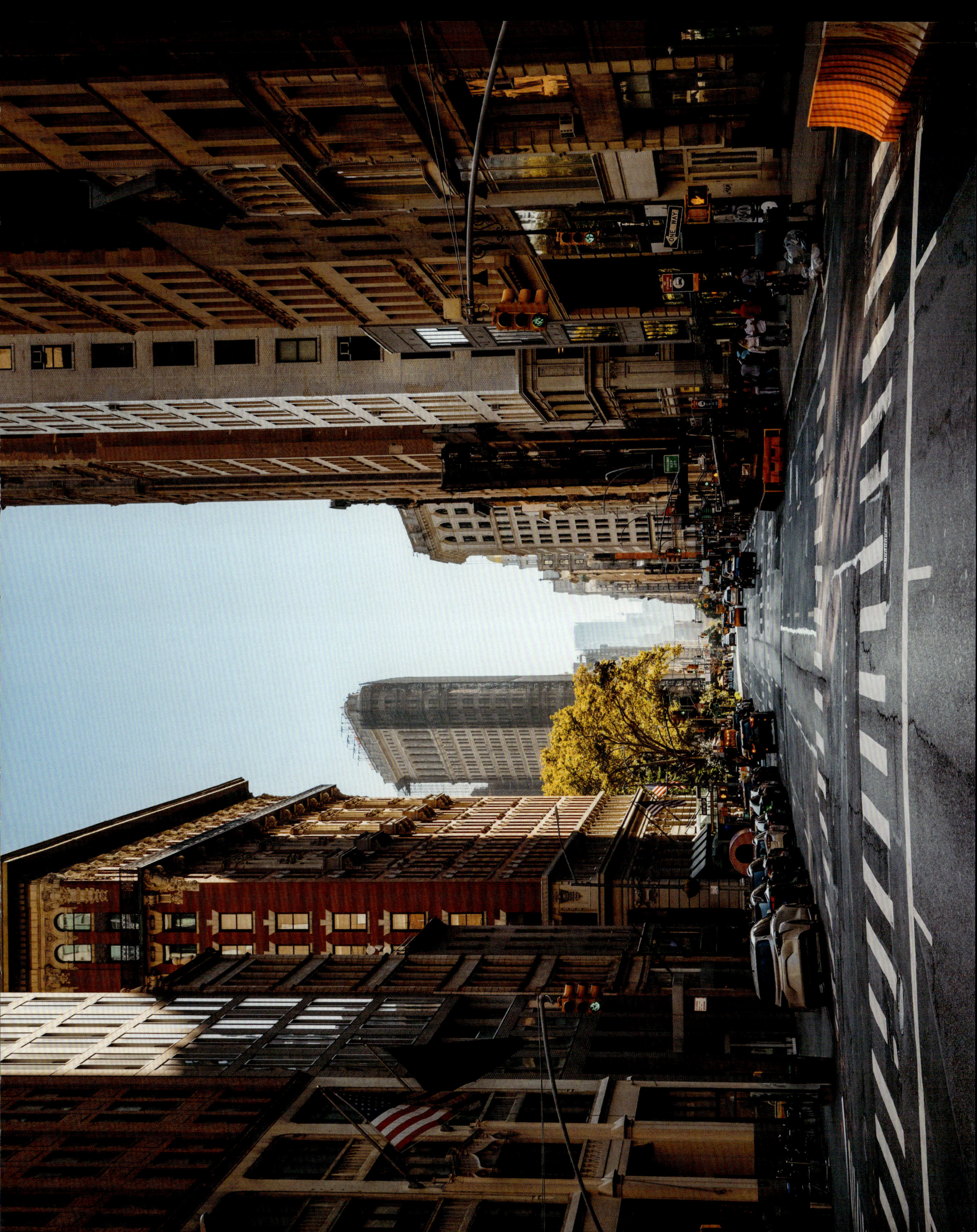

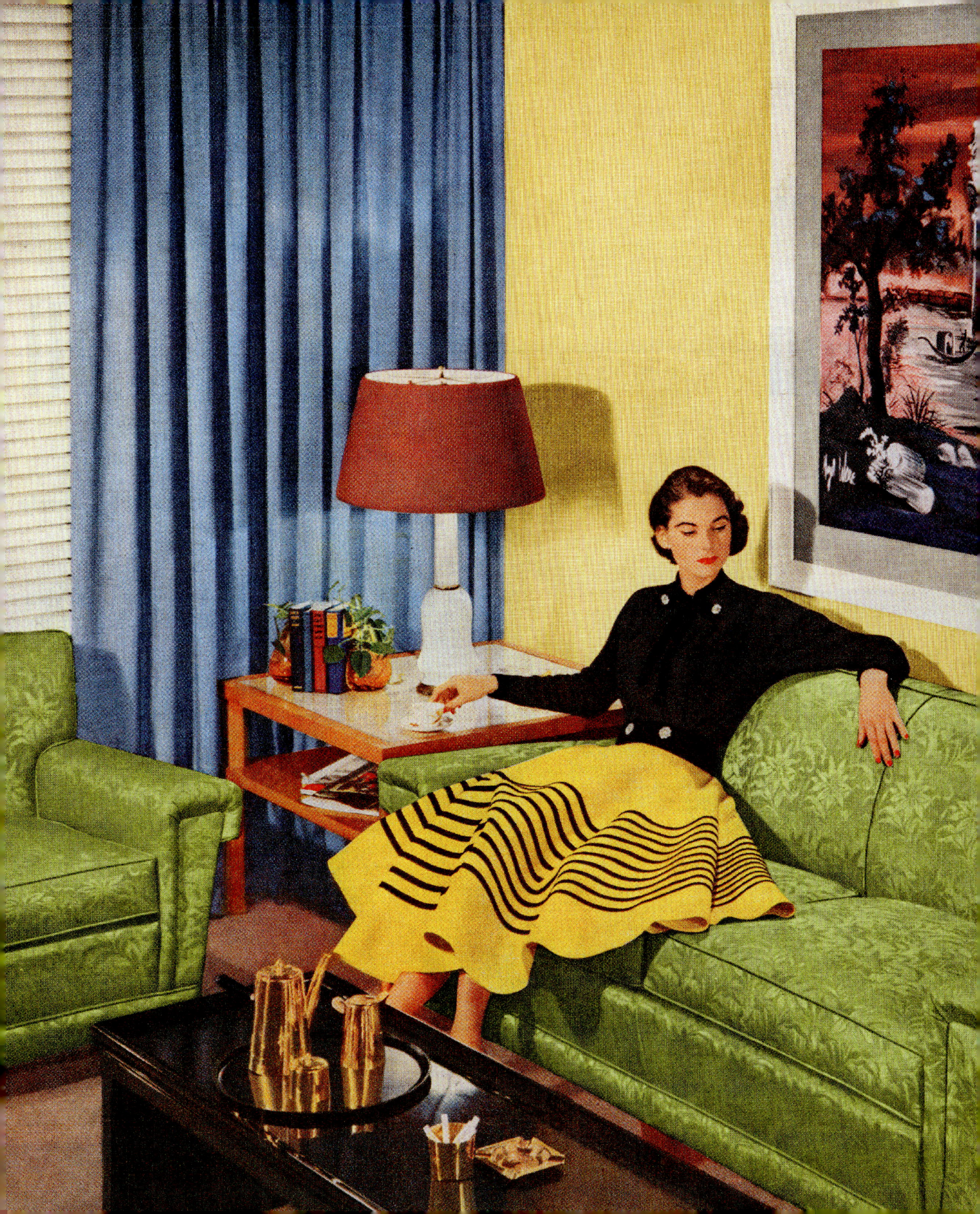

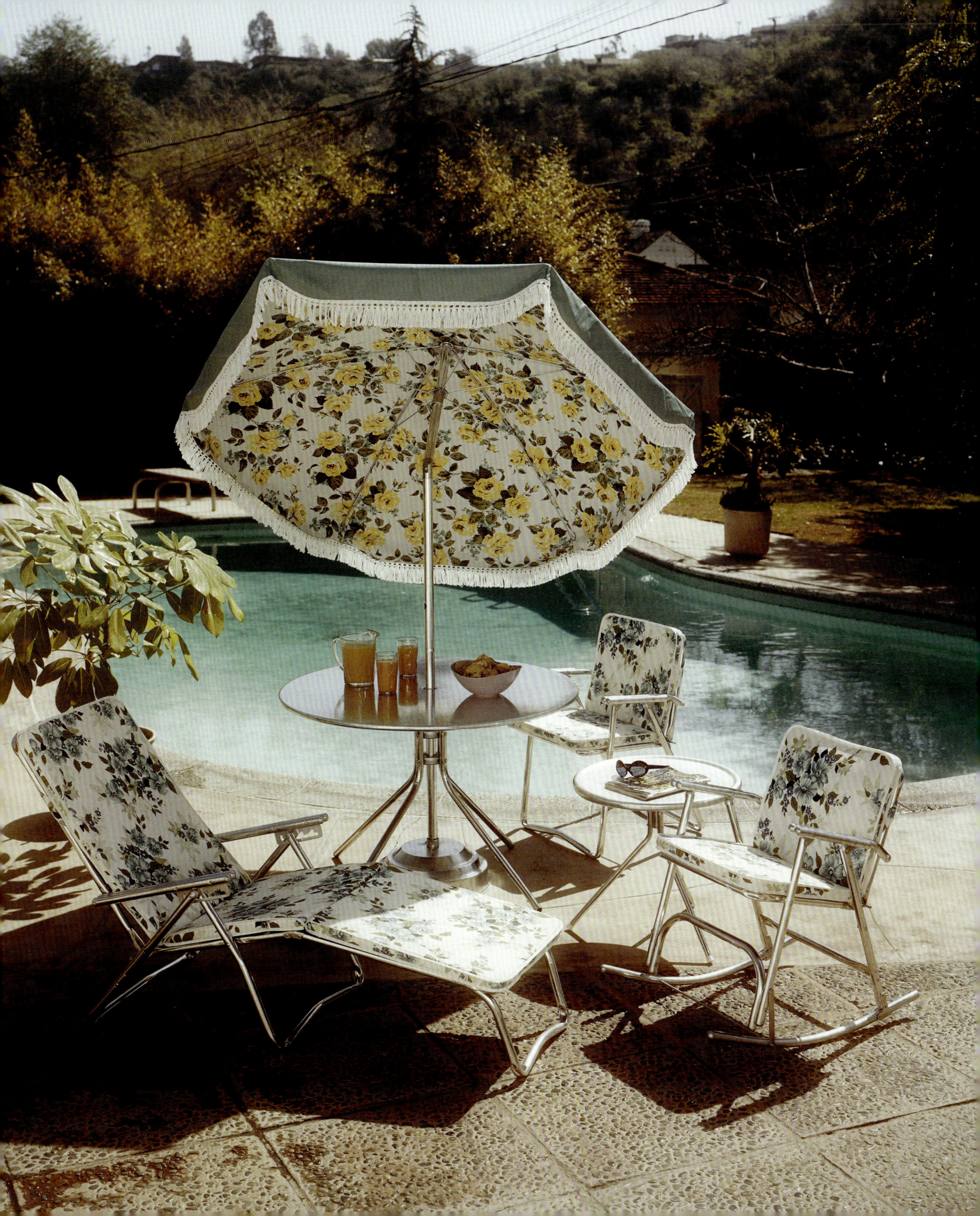

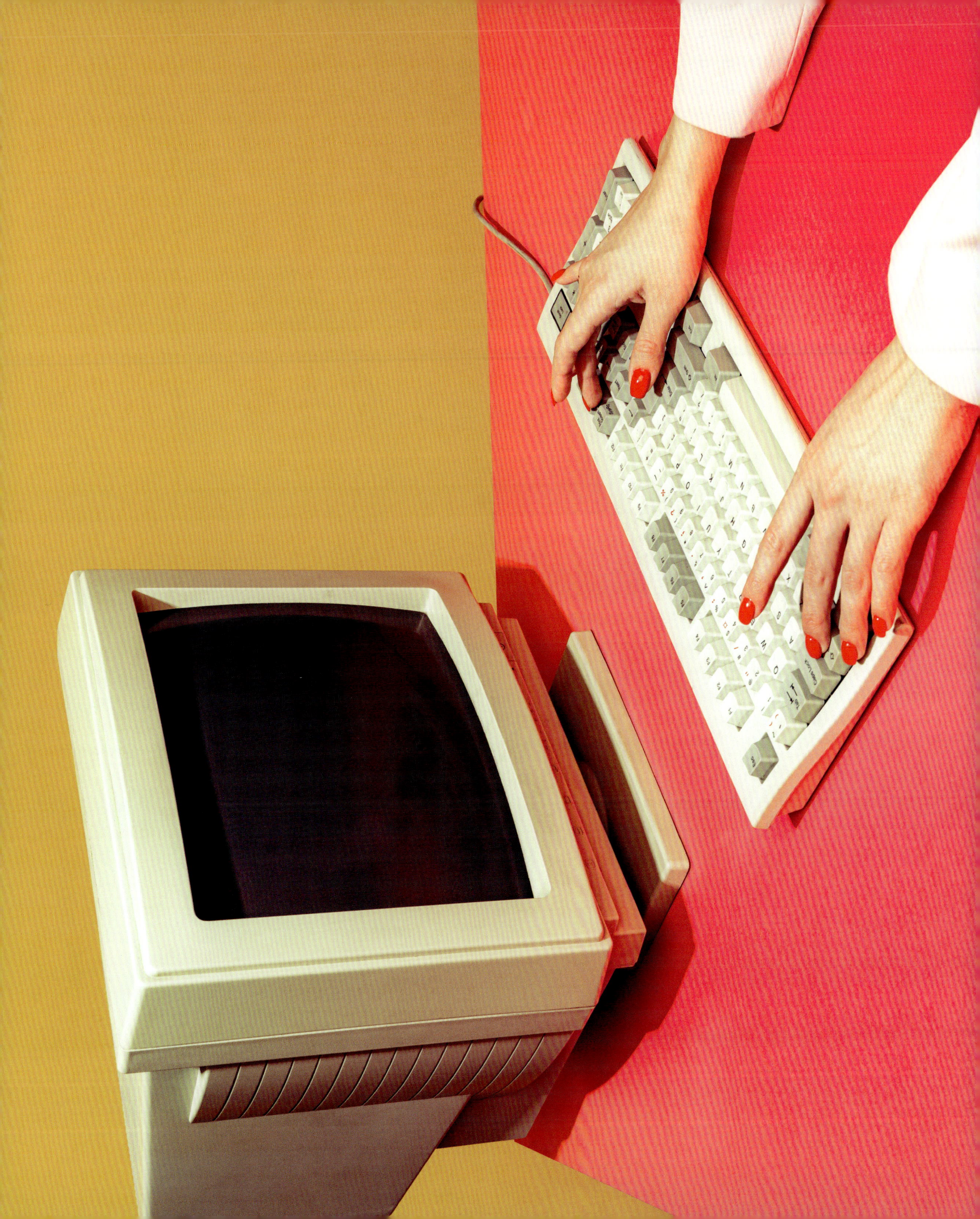

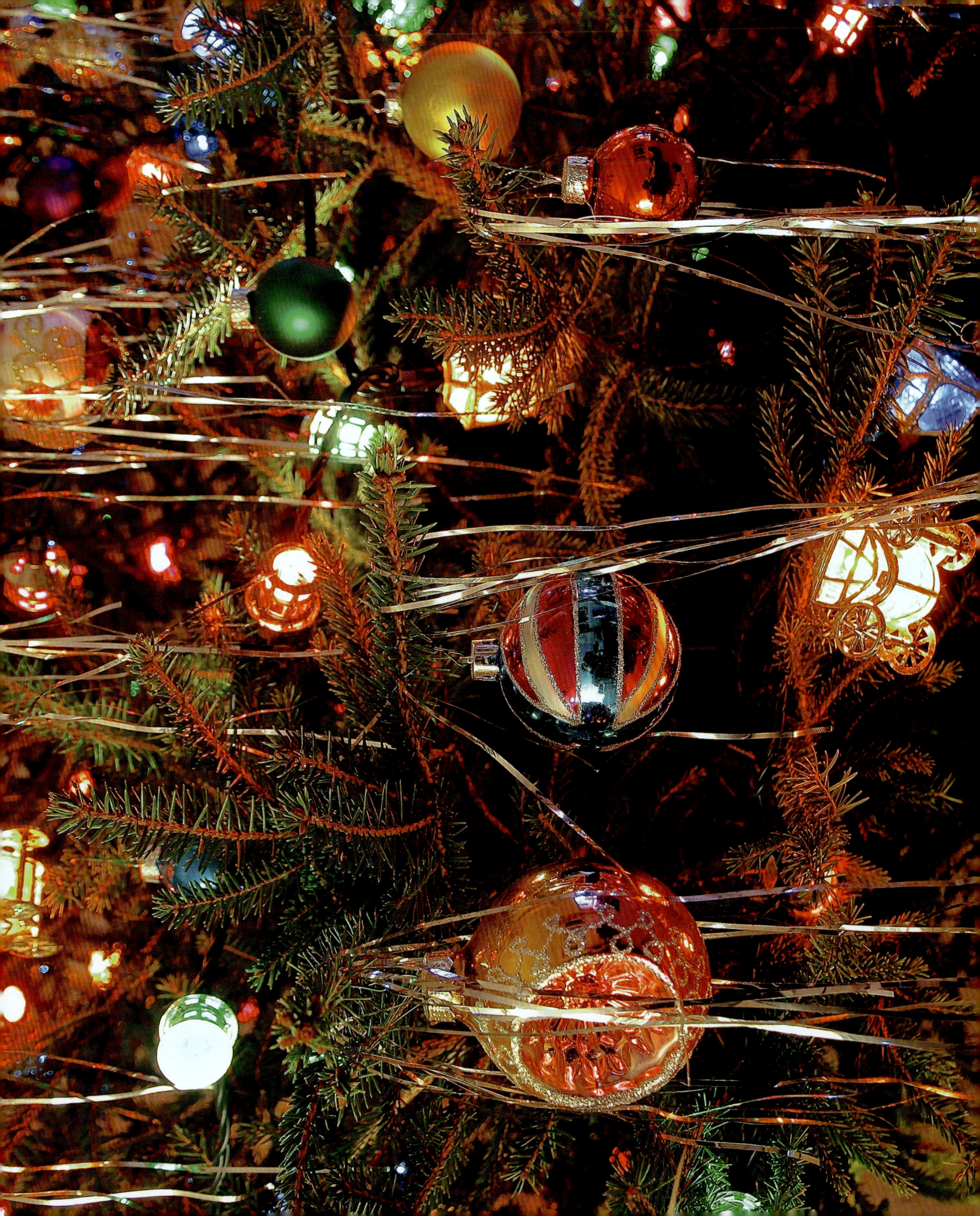

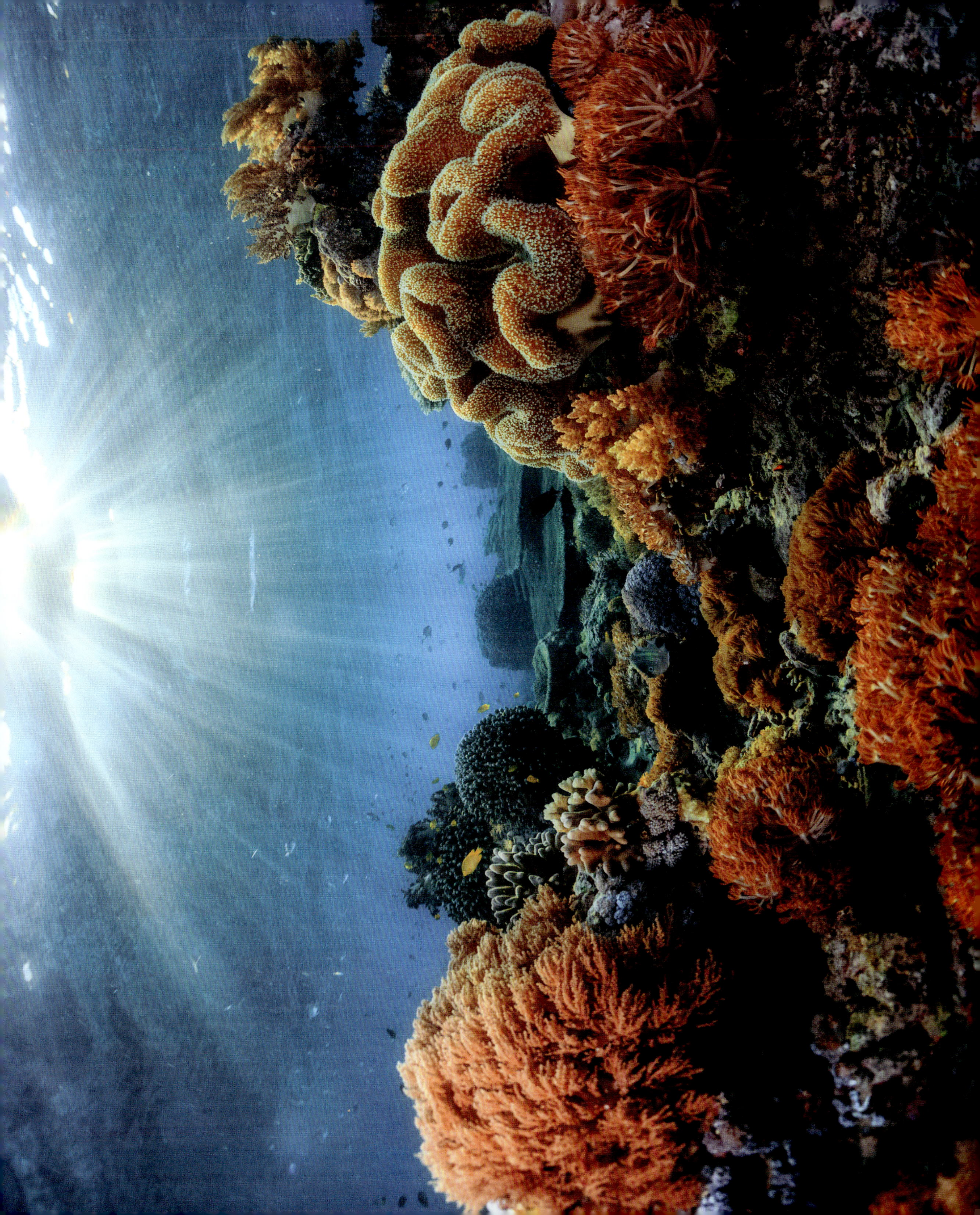

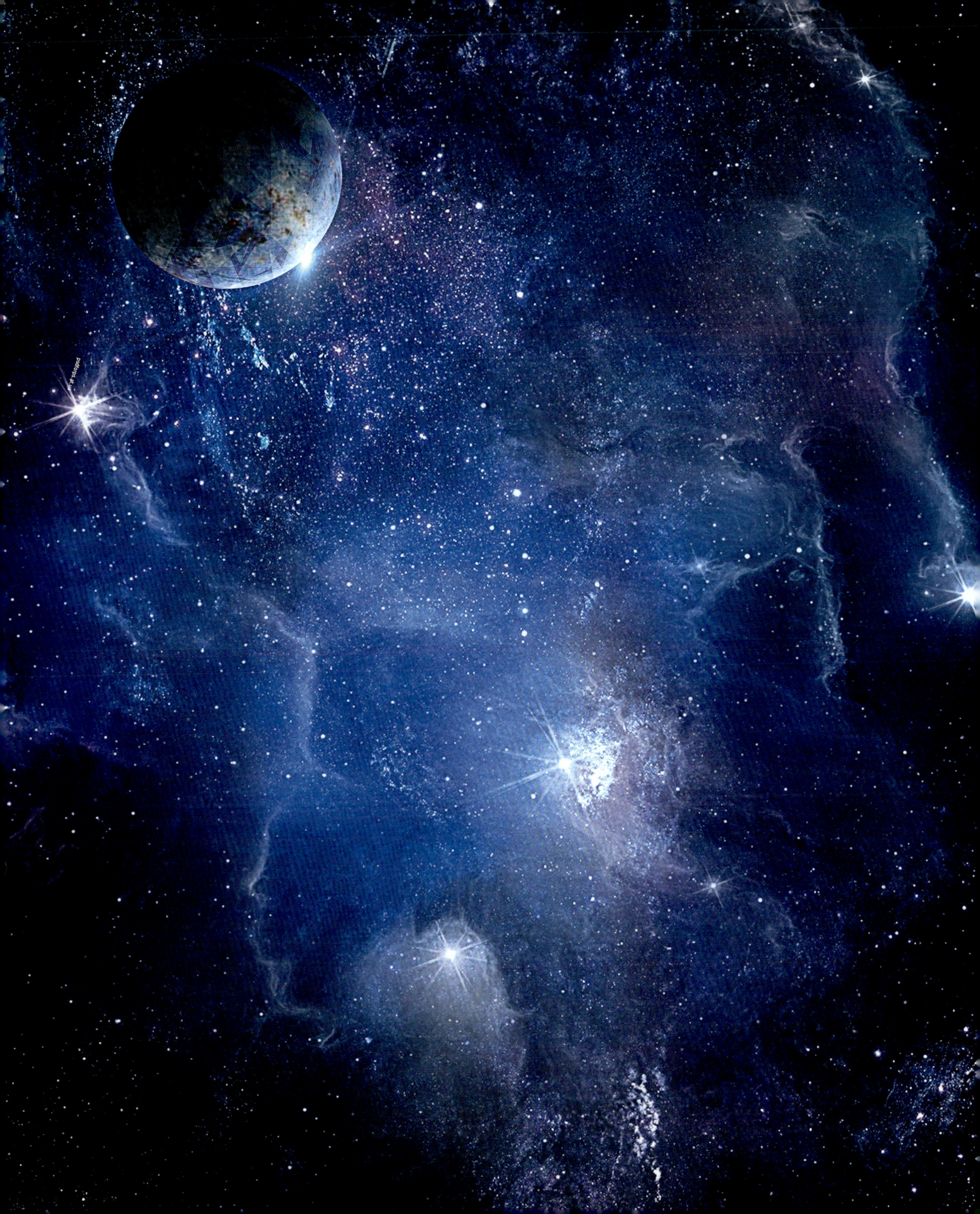

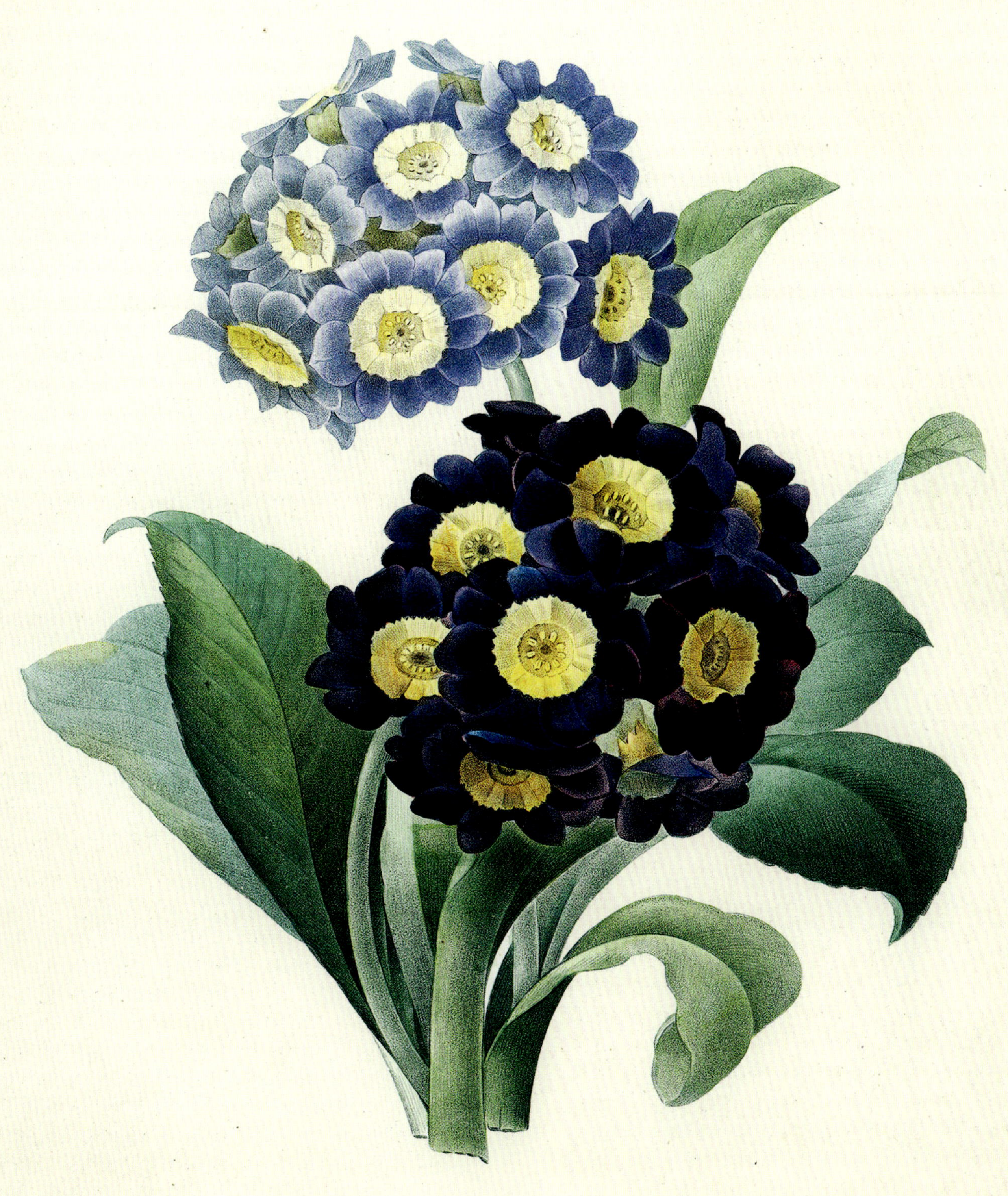

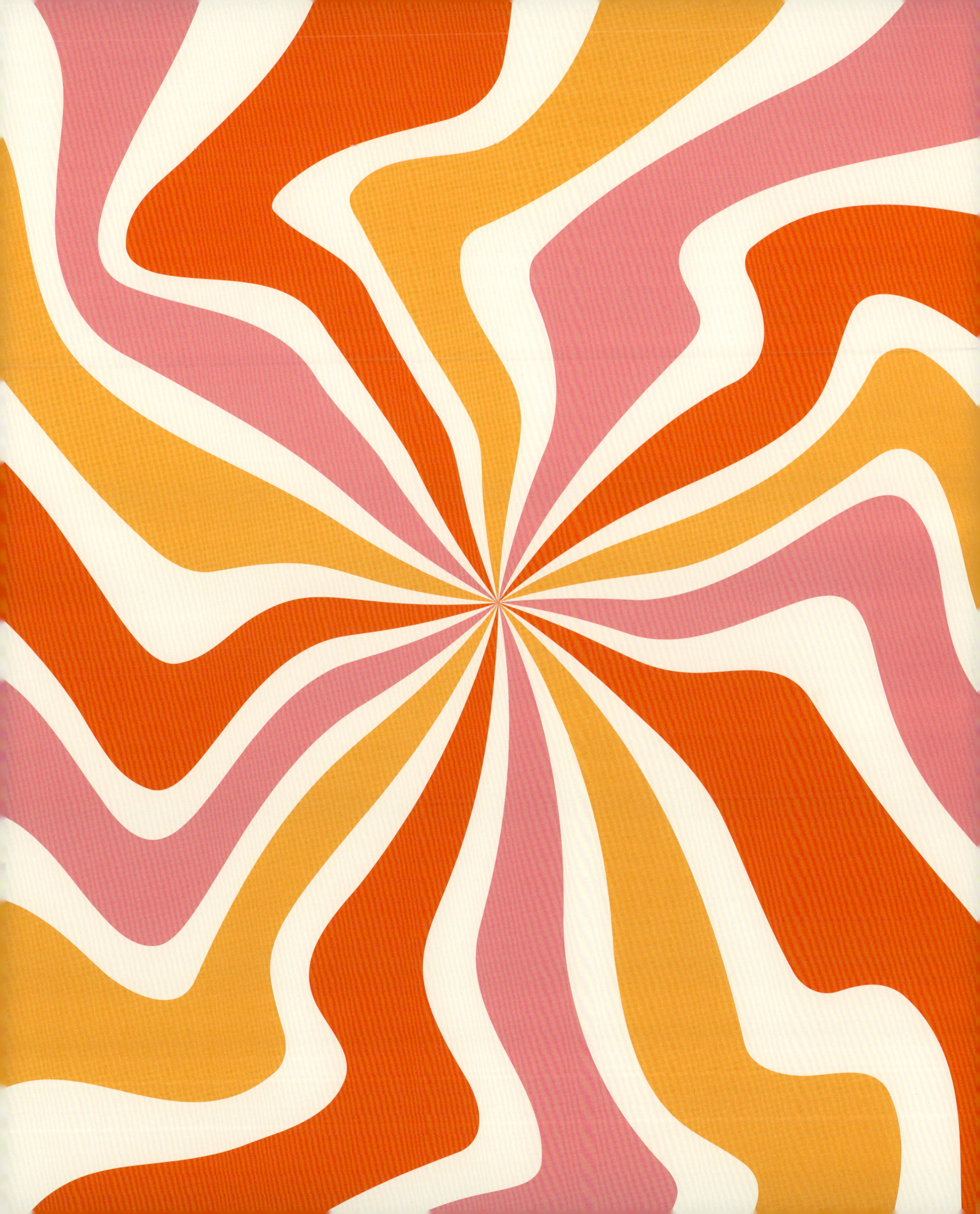

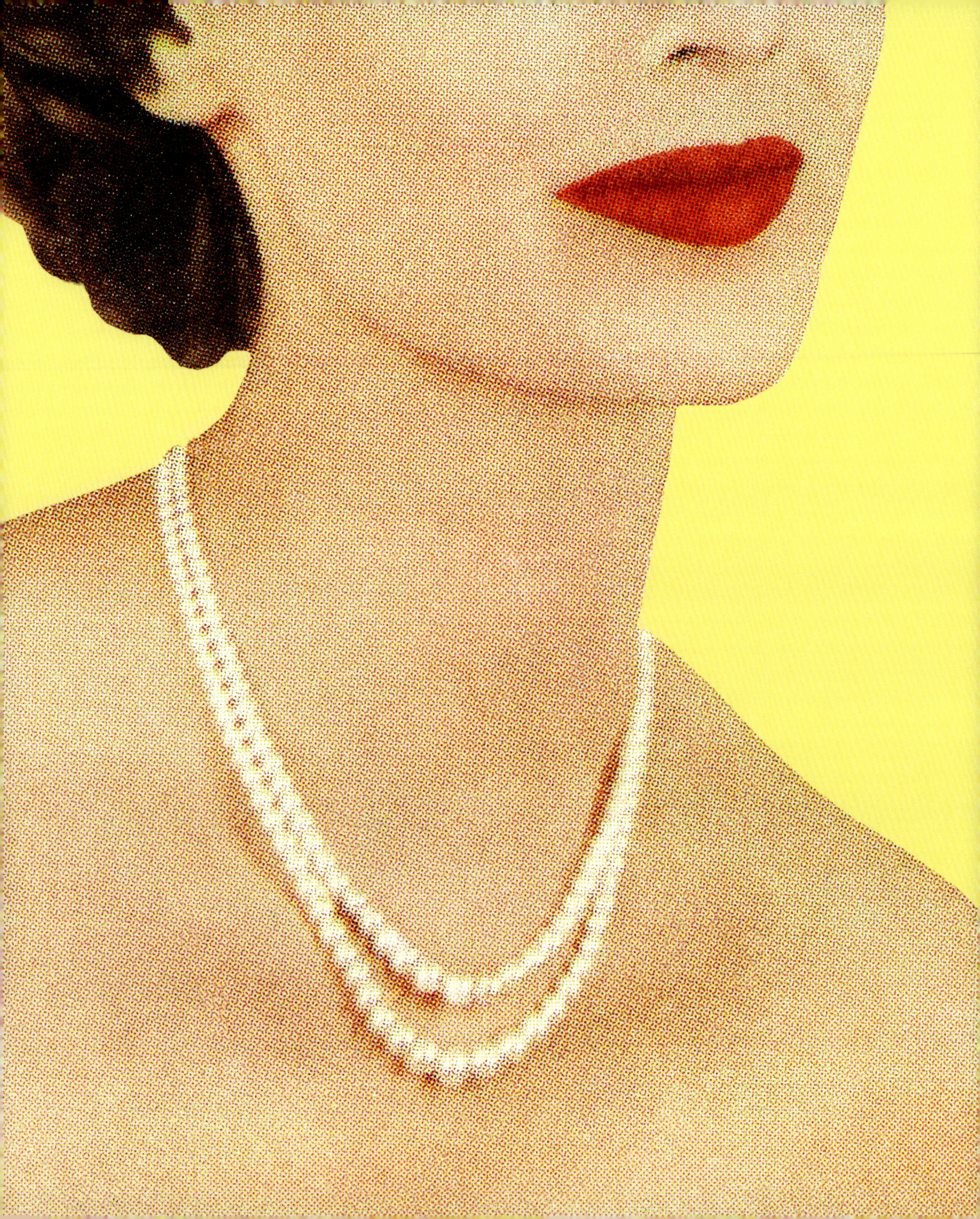

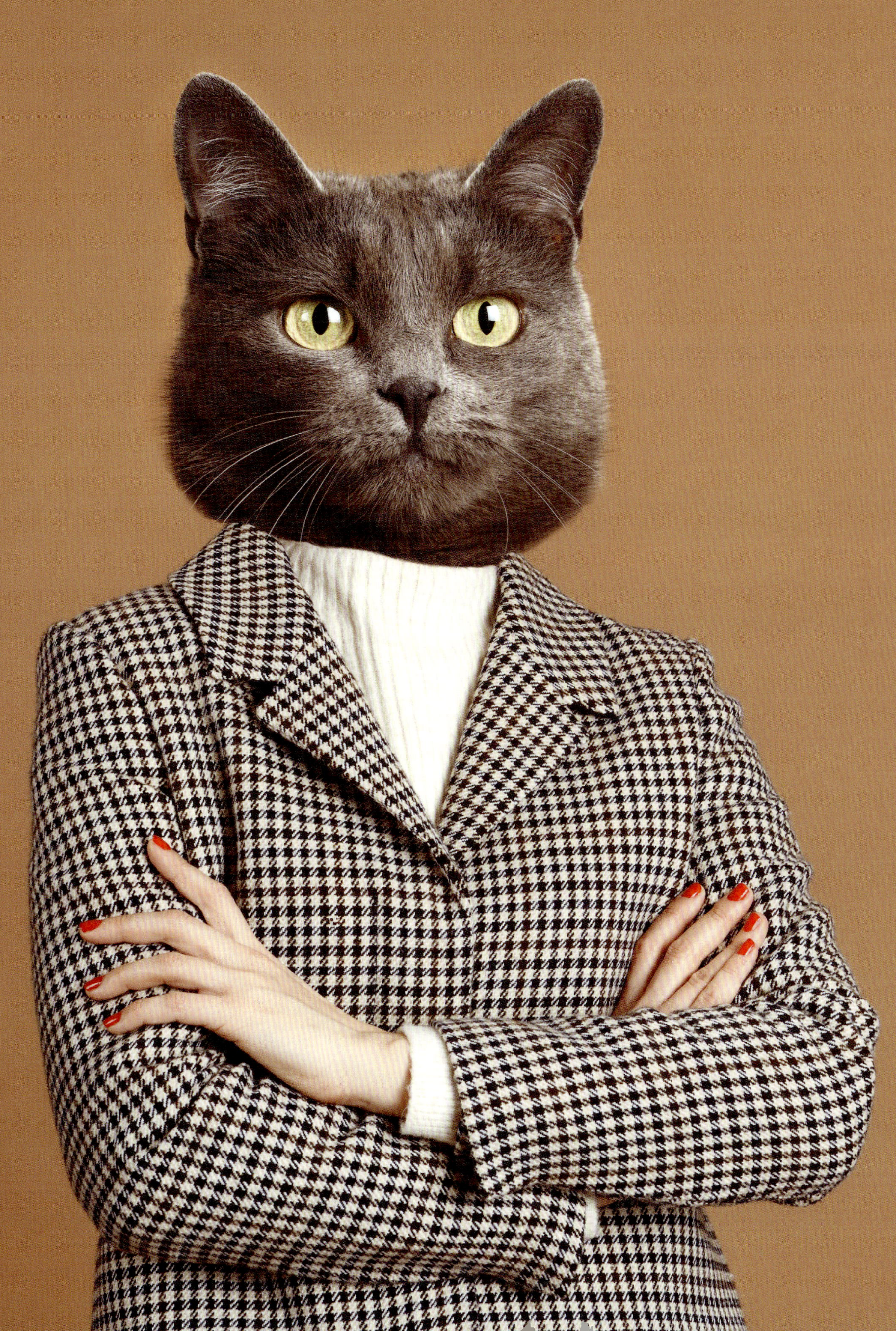